SPIRITS WALK WITH ME

AN ENOCHIAN ODYSSEY

Jonathan Back

British Library Cataloguing-in-publication data.
A catalogue record for this book is available from the
British Library.

Published by Rosden Ltd
372 Old Street
London
EC1V 9LT
(020) 70339992

First published 2010

ISBN 9780955888212

CHAPTER ONE

Our magickal circle delineated by tea lights, Paul and I stood within it, chanting the name of the entity we hoped to call forth. We were staying in an old stone cottage about two miles from Glastonbury, and this was the culmination of our trip, an attempt to summon a spirit that had previously only existed in my imagination. His name was Dr Funk, and I conceived of him as a dark and dirty groovster, a Pan-like figure with plenty of sway in his hips and lust in his eyes. He was hot – and I was about to find out just how goddam smokin' hot he was . . .

With a backing track of heavy, funky rhythms, we called his name whilst holding in our minds the sigil that I had created to tag him with. When I started to smell smoke I felt my heart begin to race . . . it was happening! I had had my eyes closed, but I turned to look at Paul, whose scared grin showed that he had smelt the smoke, too. I closed my eyes and continued to chant. The smell of smoke grew stronger, and before long I began to feel heat, too. I managed to maintain my position for another couple of minutes, but by then the heat was so intense – it felt like the house was on fire. I turned around. The house *was* on fire! At least the sofa just beyond the perimeter of our circle was alight, sending flames a good three foot into the air, along with clouds of choking black smoke.

'Fuck!' I bellowed.

We knew we had to act quickly, but at the same time there was something wonderful about the sight of those red and orange flame tentacles as they rose into the air. Eventually we managed to shake ourselves from our hypnotic state. I ran to the kitchen and quickly filled up a saucepan with water, then rushed back and threw it on the fire. It took a good few minutes before we had doused the flames, and then we stood together, breathing heavily and smelling damp ash.

After we had recovered from the shock of what had happened, we began to consider *how* it had happened. Had Dr Funk showed up with a can of petrol in hand and mischief in his heart? Or was there a more prosaic explanation? It was Paul who pointed out that one of the tea lights that had formed our circle was missing. We pushed the sofa back, and discovered it had been inadvertently kicked under the piece of furniture. Thereby starting the fire. I think we both felt a little bit happy and a little bit sad at this discovery. Relieved, because we could go to bed without worrying that a mad spirit was running amok in our cottage; disappointed that we hadn't just witnessed the greatest act of evocation since the days of Solomon. It was Paul's view that a stray foot had propelled the tea light under the sofa without conscious awareness, and that this could explain a lot of so-called magickal acts: we weren't consciously faking things or trying to deceive ourselves, but in performing the ritual we had given permission to a more primitive part of our minds 'to have some fun'.

There may be some truth in this idea, but the story isn't quite over. We came clean to the owner of the cottage the next morning about our 'mishap', and he was understandably annoyed that he had a pair of pyromaniacs staying in his property. Two days after our return to London I received a letter from the owner, expressing alarm at the state in which we had left the cottage. He must be mistaken, I thought. Ashamed at the destruction of the sofa, Paul and I had spent a couple of hours cleaning and tidying before we left. For a couple of guys, we did a damn good job of getting that place spic and span. The letter informed me that the owner had discovered 'slime' on the kitchen work surfaces, faeces smeared on some of the walls, and that there was a dreadful smell throughout the whole property.

One thing is certain, and that is that the cottage was not in the state described when we left. That leaves several possibilities. One is that the owner made the whole thing up. Extremely unlikely, as we had already forfeited our bond due to the damage the sofa had suffered. Another possibility is that someone – someone who walks around with a bucket of slime – broke into the property and created the mess described. This seems unlikely. Vandalism of cottages in rural Somerset doesn't sound like a common crime. The third possibility is that Dr Funk didn't leave the property with us (we didn't do any sort of banishing) and that even if he hadn't set fire to the sofa, he decided to make his presence known after our departure. In the years since, I've often been tempted to contact the owner, to find out whether he has experienced any further strange happenings in the property . . .

My Glastonbury adventure is just one of a host of 'experiences of otherness' I have had throughout my life. Before the age of eighteen the paranormal seemed to come looking for me; after reaching adulthood it was the other way around. I'm a rational sort of guy, as a degree in Economics and my abandonment at an early age of Fundamentalist Christianity would seem to attest. Nevertheless, it became apparent to me very early on in my life that the scientific view of reality was not complete, and that even if the world wasn't created in seven days, magickal events *were* happening to people on a regular basis.

Accepting the reality of spiritual dimensions creates a huge dilemma for someone that likes explanations for things. The simple question, 'Are spirits real?' gave me headaches when I sought an answer to it. To begin with, defining the terms 'spirits' and 'real' seemed far more problematic than I might have hoped. Is anything 'real' in a definitive and perfectly objective sense? A tree consisting of leaves and bark is real on the physical plane, but is it real on the imaginary plane? Likewise, the image of a tree that I hold in my mind must be real on some level of existence, but on that level is a sap-and-cellulose tree real? And what are we talking about exactly when we refer to 'spirits'? Is this a term that should have been retired a century ago?

The Goetic texts tell us of spirits that we can command to do our bidding, but are they anything other than personifications of categories of instinct or impulse? Then again, if these spirits have a name, are talked about, and can be summoned, then they must be real in one sense, even if they can't be traced to a particular level of the astral plane and surprised at home in their slippers. And yet maybe they can be . . .

In looking for answers to these questions, I thought I might do worse than looking at the writings of masters of the occult that have gone before. I was initially excited when I read in Aleister Crowley's 'Liber O': 'In this book it is spoken of the Sephiroth and the paths; of Spirits and of Conjurations; of Gods, Spheres, Planes, and many other things which may or may not exist. It is immaterial whether they exist or not; by doing certain things certain results will follow; students are most earnestly warned against attributing any objective reality or philosophical validity to any of them.' This seemed to free me from the necessity of believing in disincarnate entities; I could adopt a more psychological approach to magick. But then as I read more Crowley, I came across his account of the transmission of 'The Book of the Law' by Aiwass. Crowley seemed to be disobeying his own advice in very much attributing objective reality to Aiwass. I was confused!

So what do I think? I'll save my final conclusions for a later chapter, but here are some initial observations – observations that are elaborated on throughout this book. Firstly, I think that we need to be cautious about attributing objective reality to *anything*. The term may even be meaningless. Quantum mechanics has led scientists to conjecture that there may be an infinite number of parallel universes, that reality is probabilistic and only 'crystallises' when it is observed, that particles can exist in two places at the same time, and, in the view of Amit Goswami and others, that there is no reality independent of consciousness. So the correct response to someone who says, 'Yes, but spirits aren't real' could very well be, 'No, but nor are you!'

Leaving aside the quagmire semantics can drag us into, and scientific speculation that requires a PhD in physics to indulge in, I think it is still valid the try and reach a conclusion about the nature of the spirits we seek to conjure and communicate with.

We have to have some notion of what they represent in order to believe (or not) in our magick, and their degree of autonomy also determines how seriously we need to take things like banishing. Do we see a psychotherapist or a fellow mage if a magickal operation goes badly wrong? Nothing may be 'real', but we live in a world where we have to at least treat things as having different levels of reality. The tax demand I receive from my tax office may not be 'real' in some senses, but I'll still behave as if it is.

In considering issues of 'reality' and 'being' I am reminded of Chapter One, Verse One of the Gospel of St. John: 'In the beginning was the word, and the word was God.' The act of naming something – providing the word – is more than just a way of distinguishing it from something else; it's a creative act, and in a sense anything that has a name has an existence, even if is a 'subjective-objective' one. This ties in with the quantum mechanical idea that looking at something 'collapses' its probability wave, bringing it into reality. In the case of my Dr Funk, just providing this hitherto non-existent entity with a name brought him into existence, and further imaginative work that was done to build up a clear picture of him was secondary to this initial act. The esoteric significance of naming explains the importance placed on the act of baptism, which in most societies has a meaning far deeper than differentiating Jim from James.

Thinking along these lines about a year ago resulted in me conducting a little experiment. As I describe in detail later, I am interested in furthering John Dee's work on angelic magick, and to this end I decided I needed some help. What, I wondered, if there were little pointers that might help me search in the right direction? I decided that there *were* (or would be), and that they were called *chorkles*. Chorkles, as I conceived of them, were patches of colour, sky or electric blue, and they pointed to, or indicated, lines of enquiry that would be useful in my Enochian research. That was it. They were named, and they came into existence at that same moment. I immediately forgot about them, and it was some three days later, sitting on the bus, that I noticed a T-shaped no-through-road sign, which had a background that was in just this same blue colour. I didn't immediately think 'chorkles'. It was only after the thought 'why am I thinking about this road sign?' arose that I realised I had seen a chorkle! As I will explain in due course, this chorkle was pointing me in just the right direction.

In discussing whether spirits are more than a meaningless mental construct, an area that repays examination is whether interaction with disincarnate entities leads to physical phenomena, and this is a question I will return to throughout this book. If spirits are purely 'parts of our brain', then we would not expect communion with them to lead to any changes in our environment. Although spirits are never going to appear in a cloud of sulphur, cracking the ceiling of the magician's temple as they expand to full height, it *is* the case that magickal operations can result in physical anomalies. This can be as mild as electromagnetic interference, all the way through to violent poltergeist-like activity. I remember during one Enochian scrying session seeing one of the candles I had lit burn down to nothing in about two minutes (this a candle that would normally provide illumination for thirty six hours). For about six hours after the working, whenever I lit a match, the match head would explode, not simply ignite – and this even after I had switched to a friend's box of matches. Interestingly, it was a fiery Aethyr (the 6th) I had been exploring!

The practice of creating a body of light in order to explore astral realms is intriguing in examining the whole objectivity/subjectivity of spirits question. The technique is simple to describe, but requires perseverance to perform successfully. The occultist, after stilling his mind through breathing exercises and the relaxation of the body, imagines in his mind's eye a simulacrum, or double, of his flesh-and-bones body, the latter normally seated or standing facing the practitioner. With time, this astral body attains a sufficient degree of crispness and reality tone, after which the magician's consciousness can be transferred to the double. Sights and impressions can then be received whilst looking through the double's eyes that are accurate in terms of both physical and astral reality. What I find interesting about this exercise is that it involves creating an 'object' of the 'subject', thereby forcing a transcendent degree of perception. I believe a new paradigm of magickal understanding needs to emerge which is not fixated on the 'objective' or 'subjective' quality of experience, because magickal reality transcends both. Herein lies an explanation for why magickal experience will never be verifiable by scientific or strictly objective means – it goes beyond it, and therefore cannot be accurately assessed by its current techniques and methods.

So buckle up and enjoy the ride! In the following chapters I will be exploring the ideas raised in the preceding paragraphs, using the time line of my magickal experiences to structure and give context to the main ideas introduced in the book. A key aim will be to explore the nature of spirits – modelling them if you like – and the spirits that will feature most prominently will be those that appear in Enochian magick – the angels of John Dee and Edward Kelly. Some of the time I'll be 'jamming' – there'll be plenty of free association and leaps of thought – and some of the time I'm going to sound quite serious and sober – but don't worry, it'll be me throughout! I devote three chapters to my Enochian experiences, which represent the most exciting area of my magickal research to date, and which have been incredibly revealing in terms of probing and exploring the spirit world. At the end of Book One I present a theory of the spirit world, an expansion of the ideas expressed above that uses my metaphysical adventures as a backdrop and testing ground. Hopefully at the very least readers will find something to provoke thought there. Book One is the 'main course' of this offering. Book Two is the 'dessert' and comprises a short story I have entitled 'The Stella of Revealing'. It's part parody, part instructional fable, and totally crazy. I hope you enjoy it.

CHAPTER TWO

If you mention the country 'Yemen' to most people nowadays, they will either give you a blank stare or mumble something about Al-Qaeda. Shame on such ignorance! This is the land that gave us the Queen of Sheba – King Solomon's consort – and the strain of Islam currently in the ascendant in present day Saudi Arabia. Furthermore, if your thing is either daggers in scabbards, or psychoactive leaves that you can chew, then Yemen is the place for you, for all the men walk around with the former, and the latter is in abundance in the form of a plant called khat.

It was certainly the place for my parents, but not because of the trippy leaves, daggers or the Queen of Sheba. No, they were drawn there because of the state religion – Islam – and their business was the Missionary Business – the Christian Missionary Business to be precise. I have heard a few theories as to why people are drawn to evangelism, ranging from psychological disorders to wanderlust, but whatever the reason in the case of my parents, they travelled to the Yemen a year before my birth. As we returned to Australia when I was three, most my memories of the country are sketchy, though I do recall the aftermath of sitting on an ant's nest.

What I do most certainly remember are the nightmares that I had on an almost nightly basis, from the age of two right up until I was about seven. My father has a theory about their cause, and whilst I can't say for sure whether he is right, it makes an intriguing story. During our time in Yemen we lived in the small town of Jibla, right opposite the local marabout, or wise man. I gather it was accidental that we should end up so located, but then it would be just like my father to 'get in the face of the enemy'. This wise man would have been doubly bad in my father's books, as not only was he a Muslim, but as a spell-caster and fortune-teller, he was a goddam Devil worshipper to boot.

I don't remember any of this, but apparently I struck up a friendship with the marabout's son. His name was Ali. We played daily, with him normally coming over to my place, and me occa-sionally going over to his (supervised by the Yemeni woman my parents employed to help out). The relationship blossomed, and I guess after six months I was probably picking up the odd word of Arabic. I don't know whether either of us had much in the way of toys, but I suppose at the age we were, sticks and cups are just as fun. Everything went wonderfully until one day we had a dreadful argument whilst playing at Ali's house. Nobody knows what it was about, but I was so riled that I pushed Ali violently. One-and-a-half year olds are well adapted to falling over, but unfortunately my companion was standing next to a hoe-like tool when I gave him an almighty shove. The boy fell onto the implement, and ended up badly gashing his forehead. There was no serious injury to him, but there *was* a lot of blood. Ali's father, who was in the house at the time, was enraged at the harm I had caused his son, and went over immediately to remonstrate with my father. Ali was the man's only son – he had five daughters – and in a culture that places such importance on a male heir I guess the marabout thought he had suffered a fate about as bad as having his testicles mangled.

I don't think the man thought that I had deliberately planned to injure his son, but he wanted something from my father beyond the simple apology he was given. Perhaps a *huge* apol-ogy would have sufficed, or a gift of some sort. Whatever it was the marabout was after, he didn't get it, and the man stormed off after berating my father for a few minutes. From that day onwards I was forbidden by the Yemeni from playing with Ali, Ali's father refused to speak to me and my family . . . and the regular nightmares started. My father describes me waking within an hour of falling asleep practically every night, scream-ing at a volume my parents could scarcely believe a child of my age was capable of. Being taken into my parents bed and having the lights switched on was not guaranteed to settle me straight away, and I would sometimes stay awake for hours, whimpering at the memory of whatever my dream had involved.

Though I don't remember my nightmares in Yemen, I do most certainly remember them as they continued after our return to Australia. I recall that they always involved a particular house – a house that was unlike any that I have ever visited, but which was nonetheless very familiar. It felt old – ancient even – and was made of stone, with little in the way of furnishings. Above all it was dark, always dark, and the sense of oppression I felt whilst in this dream environment was almost impossible to describe. In my young mind it was the 'bad place', and the fact that I couldn't articulate what made it bad only seemed to add to its horror.

I might be inclined to dismiss any link between the marabout and these nightmares – my father's theory – if it weren't for another baffling occurrence that happened towards the tail end of these night terrors. At the age of about six, for a period of ten days or so, there was an odour that followed me around wherever I went. The smell was of urine and freshly cut plants – chlorophyll I suppose. Before you wonder – no, I hadn't done pee-pee down my leg, and was then wondering what this strange smell could be. I was toilet trained by this age, changed my clothes daily, and bathed regularly. I remember complaining to my parents about the smell, and them running through a check-list of possible explanations for it without success. The smell was oppressive, in the same way as my nightmares were. It wasn't just that it isn't pleasant having the scent of urine tickling your nostrils all day long – there was a sense, strongly felt, that the smell was following me, and that it was somehow sentient – or belonged to something that was. As strong as the stench was to me, no-one else could detect it. Smell is the most primitive of our senses, and the most closely connected with our unconscious, and just as my nightmares were manifestations of my unconscious mind, so I wonder whether this odour was the primitive part of my brain's way of telling me that there was something 'shadowing' me. If so, does this cast light on the way spirits manifest?

So was the marabout responsible? Of course, I can't be certain, but I'm inclined to say 'yes'. It may have not even been deliberate, but perhaps in the aftermath of his son's accident a particularly virulent thoughtform was generated, which trailed me for the next few years. Some who know me might say it hasn't to this day been banished. You can make your own mind up after you have read the rest of this book . . .

Returning to Yemen for a second, there is an amusing story told by my father about one of his less successful evangelising missions whilst he lived in the country. He and a couple of other missionaries were spending a couple of days in a remote, mountainous part of the country, visiting people who I guess had probably never met Westerners before. Over tea with some village elders, they broached the subject of Jesus, and how these peoples' lives really would be made infinitely better if they accepted him as their Lord and Saviour. One of the men nodded patiently as he was hearing this, then proceeded to explain that he knew all about this Jesus! Yes sir! Apparently the story of the foretelling of Jesus' birth by their ancestors had been passed down the generations amongst these people . . . as my father was talking to descendants of the original Wise Men! This story sounds in some ways hard to believe, but I know my father, for all his faults, would not have made it up. Which leaves two possibilities – that these Yemenis were making it up, or that it's true! It *is* the case that Yemen is given as one of the possible origins of the legendary stargazers.

My father's theory is that since this run-in with the marabout, 'I haven't haven't been quite right'. Whether this is the case or not, I must confess to wondering whether the man had any influence on my subsequent occult career. Is living in proximity to a man of spiritual powers at a young age likely to incline a person to follow a spiritual path?

A couple of months after the 'smelly ghost' episode, I had another strange experience. This one was interesting in that it foreshadowed an event that happened in Africa when I was fifteen, which will be described in the next chapter. It was evening, and I was lying in bed. As I recall, my step-mother had just read my brother and I a bedtime story, and we were probably a couple of minutes from 'lights out'. Suddenly, I was hit by the most gripping sense of fear imaginable. As someone who has in the past suffered from panic attacks, I can state unequivocally that it was of a magnitude several orders greater than these. Moreover, whereas with a panic attack there tends to be a focus for the panic – 'I hate the Underground', 'I can't breathe', etc., with this attack I couldn't say what was scaring me so badly. If forced to explain what was happening, I would have to say that it felt like I was about to undergo annihilation – not just physical annihilation, but the destruction of my soul as well. Looking back on the event, and with the benefit of a much bigger vocabulary than I possessed aged six, I would describe what happened as feeling as if my spiritual double was being squeezed by some sort of entity on that plane, and that I was feeling the ramifications of this in my flesh-and-bones body. What made all of this so petrifying was that I couldn't verbalise any of this. I was beside myself with fear, but couldn't be any more specific than 'I feel bad' in describing what I was experiencing. My step-mother interpreted all of this in spiritual terms, her take on things being that I was experiencing the presence of God. No wonder I never became a born again Christian. If that was what the presence of God felt like, I wanted nothing to do with it!

Another aspect of my Yemen years which sometimes makes me scratch my head is the legendary origin of the Three Wise Men as being from this country, and my own fascination with astrology. When I talk about astrology I certainly don't mean the tabloid-paper-sun-sign-variety, nor even the Western (Tropical) say-what-you-like-about-someone's-personality-because-they'll-always-latch-on-to-something-to-support-your-comments variety The only use for newspaper astrology is to wipe your bottom with if you run out of T.P., and Western psychologically-based astrology is just so much waffle and tea-leaf-gazing without psychic ability. No, astrology to me is the full-strength variety, Vedic astrology, which uses the sidereal zodiac, and has the power to amaze with its predictive power. If ever a demonstration of the truth of the Hermetic maxim 'As Above, So Below' were needed, real astrology provides it.

The sort of accuracy Vedic astrological techniques are capable of providing, by someone skilled in their use, would be forecasts of time of death in an otherwise healthy person to within a week, or an assessment of likely career based on nothing but birth data, with a high degree of specificity, i.e. 'an interior designer who works predominantly with people living in period buildings and castles'. Richard Houck, who wrote the fabulous 'The Astrology of Death' and did much to popularise Vedic techniques in the West, ran an astrological consultancy for many years, and with many of his clients was happy to offer a 'double your money back if my predictions are wrong' guarantee. Talk about putting your money where your mouth is. (He did, however, get his own date-of-death prediction wrong, an irony that I'm sure was not lost on him.)

I've always been interested in theories for the mechanism by which astrology operates. Why is 'above reflected below', and how? It has also struck me as possible that an explanation for the mechanism behind the workings of astrological principles might shed light on the 'reality' or not of spirits issue. After much thought I present my theory for the mechanism behind celestial influence. Firstly, there is no such thing as celestial influence. In our unenlightened state we fall for the traps of duality, which is responsible for the illusion of matter and time. (It's no coincidence that the two variables are often considered together by physicists). Think about it, duality gives us a 'before' and an 'after', whereas in actual fact both are meaningless concepts from a non-dualistic point of view, because in a non-dualistic state *time does not exist*. If time does not exist, then we can say that everything simultaneously has happened, is happening and will happen. If everything has already happened, there is no such thing as the prediction of the future, as there is no future. If astrology is not predicting the future when it appears to provide forecasts, what is it doing? Well, just as there is no time, there are no 'events' of the sort we seem to experience in day-to-day life. So when, say, an earthquake occurs under the influence of a T-square at a certain point in 'time', we are just seeing the juxtaposition of the illusion of an 'event' with the illusion of a celestial alignment that mirrors that event. There is no causality involved – we are just seeing 'above' mirrored in 'below', and vice-versa. Why do these 'events' align? Because everything is One, and through the art of astrology we are helped to see glimpses of Universal Oneness and the total interconnectedness of everything. With increasing enlightenment we are able to see the links between seemingly unrelated items, events and concepts. It is for a very good reason that beginning a meditational programme, or starting magickal practices, often coincides with an increase in the number of coincidences experienced. What is happening is that practices are clearing one's channels of perception, which results in us starting to see glimpses of the Oneness of everything. With greater clarity of perception we finally achieve a breakthrough into non-dual consciousness, a state that is so hard to describe because words by their very nature create duality. From the point of view of our assessment of the 'reality' of spirits, the foregoing suggests that they are an illusion, in that we are splitting and separating in conceptualising them; but of course they could be said to be nor more of an illusion than anything else!

CHAPTER THREE

My parents' missionary mania didn't end with their leaving Yemen in 1974. Oh, no. After a stint of five years back in Australia, they returned to the 'field', this time to Mali, in West Africa. I remember it being said by one missionary that on first stepping off the plane in Dakar, Senegal, she was hit by a wave of 'Satanic oppression'. What she was probably hit with was a wave of warm tropical air, which she interpreted as a cloud of fart gas from Lucifer's behind, but I didn't bother pointing this out. Though this woman was being confused by her faulty belief-system, what *is* true is that African people as a whole are much more in contact with the spirit world than we in the West. One of my abiding memories of the three years I spend in Mali is the sound of the almost nightly 'devil dances' as they were called. I never actually witnessed one of these, but I can still hear the haunting sound of women making the eerie ululating noise that accompanied them. It is very easy to understand the origins of Voodoo as being in West Africa on hearing this wailing noise, which is used to induce a possession trance.

Examples of spirit belief in Mali can be humorous. Chameleons were feared as being unlucky, and if you saw one you had to not just kill it, but stamp on its head so that its tongue was protruding from its mouth as it lay dead. Okay, that's not that humorous. There was a town not far from where we lived in North West Mali, which was considered so unlucky that it couldn't be mentioned by name – instead it was referred to as 'Washington DC'. God knows what would have happened if, in the unlikely event, a performance of Macbeth was ever put on there. One afternoon I noticed that everyone I encountered was wearing a little strip of red cloth around their wrist. On asking about this, I was told that Radio Mali had made an announcement that a swarm of devils were due to hit this part of the country at any moment, and the only protection were these bits of fabric! Oh, for the BBC to make such an announcement!

My first occult experience in Mali came during a fishing trip. We were living in a town called Kayes at the time, which is on the river Senegal. I would commonly pull tiddlers from the town's main bridge, but was eager to go for some of the larger fish I knew could be caught from more isolated spots. Asking around, it seemed that a place called 'Les Chutes De Felou' – Felou Waterfall – offered the prospect of bigger fish. One morning I set off on my parents' moped, and travelled the ten or so kilometres to this place.

There was no mistaking the spot when I arrived. A tributary of the Senegal River, rising in highlands hundreds of miles away, fell a spectacular hundred foot or so to form of a lake, perhaps a hundred yards across and surrounded almost completely by high cliffs. The river continued its course through a chasm in these cliffs, so that the effect was of a bowl of water, with waterfall on one side and escape route through a gap in the cliffs on the other. It was quite an effort to get down to the lake without tumbling headfirst, but eventually I was able to pick out a path, tottering precariously as I held my rod in one hand and a satchel in the other.

It was probably nine thirty in the morning by the time I cast my rod for the first time. The claims made about the quality of fishing there proved to be solid, and before long I was hooking into large catfish and tilapia. By noon I'd pulled a greater weight of fish out of the lake than I had out of my customary fishing spots in the previous two months. My only regret was that I had neither camera nor companion to back up what was going to be some pretty intensive boasting to my fishing chums.

I can't remember what happened in the half-hour leading up to my encounter; probably just more fishing and the occasional bite on a sandwich. What I do remember is one moment being focused intensely on my float, and the next second being attacked from behind. I say 'attacked' because that is what it was – an attack – and it took me a few seconds to realise that I hadn't been physically struck – that's what it felt like. What hit me from behind was a wave of malevolent energy, so strong it almost knocked me over. There are moments in all our lives when we feel a shiver go down our spine, and imagine there is someone staring at us from behind; the experience I felt that day was of a totally different order. My energetic system was temporarily paralysed, my whole body tingled, and I felt nauseous. I also peed myself. I can't really describe how totally ghastly the sensation I felt was as this entity grappled with me. Whatever it was, it provoked the darkest fears of which I am capable. I was scared for my life.

When I regained my composure I spun around, sure I would see some sort of ghoul standing before me. There wasn't one, but the sunlight seemed to shimmer directly in front of me as if a hologram was trying to make itself visible. If something like this happened to me today, I like to think I would try and stand firm and banish. I'm sure what would actually happen is what I did in fact do: run like bloody hell! Not giving a thought for my rod or bag, I scampered as fast as I could for the rocky slope that led up to my moped. I ascended in about a tenth of the time it took to get down, running straight for my bike when I reached the top. All the while, I was sure an invisible hand would reach out and pull me backwards. Finally I reached the moped, and tore off at top speed.

I didn't mention any of this to my family when I got home, and explained away the loss of my rod with a lie. A couple of days later one of my fishing buddies asked how my expedition had gone, and with huge relief I told him the full story. He started giggling halfway through my tale, but it was only when I had finished telling him what had happened that he explained, 'We didn't think you'd actually go out there! That place is haunted. That is where they used to carry out human sacrifices.' I was mad that I had been allowed to go to Les Chutes De Felou unaware of its history. Despite the intensity of my experience, I was also a little bit sceptical about claims of human sacrifice being carried out there. I asked around though, and everyone in Kayes over the age of ten seemed to know its reputation.

What was it? I can't say. Maybe the spirit of someone who had been sacrificed; more likely the spirit of someone who had been doing the sacrificing, judging by the heavy vibe. Why me? Maybe I'm more sensitive than most, or maybe anyone that spends time on their own in that place can expect to be buzzed. One thing that has struck me since is that spending extended periods of time staring at my float probably put me into a light trance, and that this might have amplified the strength of the episode.

What I now find so interesting about this experience is its physical component. I was buffeted by an invisible force, and with enough strength for there to be no doubt in my mind that I wasn't imagining it. If we accept this fact, the question that naturally arises is, 'What exactly buffeted me?' How could something that is invisible interact so strongly with my physical body? In thinking of answers to these questions it immediately occurred to me that something doesn't have to be visible to the naked eye to exert huge strength – gases and electricity can both flatten a person. Was my attacker a gas? Of course not. Was it using an energy similar to electricity? Possibly. Ghost hunters typically carry equipment that measures electromagnetic effects, and the application of electro-magnets to the head can cause people to have what seem like paranormal experiences. Can we then say that spirits don't have a physical body, but are able to exert influence on the material plane via the more subtle physical forces? I think this is plausible. Etheric energy would seem to be a good candidate for a force that can interact with the physical world, whilst remaining resistant to scientific observation. Etheric energy would appear to be closely associated with the electromagnetic field of the physical body.

I am reminded of a fascinating by book by Dennings and Osborne entitled 'Vodoun Fire'. In it are numerous pictures of participants at a Voodoo possession dance. Emanating from and surrounding many of the dancers are clouds of what look like red smoke. This appears to be this same etheric substance

– probably identical to the ectoplasm that mediums are meant to extrude at séances. The photographs are so shocking that the temptation to suspect forgery is natural, but at the start of the book there is an attestation by a photographic expert that, having examined the negatives, he can think of no way in which the photographs could have been faked. The book was published in the late Seventies, long before the advent of Photoshop.

So perhaps we can see spirits as having an etheric, astral, mental and spiritual counterpart, with us humans (and all physical creatures) sharing these same bodies, along with our material shell. If this is the case then they can be 'out there' and 'in our heads'. 'Out there' through the agency of their etheric presence and 'in our heads' in the sense that through our consciousness (and changes in it) we can access finer dimensions where our worlds overlap.

This occasion wasn't to be the only time that I had a strange experience whilst fishing. About two months after my visit to Les Chutes De Felou I was excitedly planning another expedition, this time to involve my father, brother, two Malian buddies, and a local priest. Okay, I hadn't invited a priest, but the thought crossed my mind that maybe I should. Our destination this time was to be a stretch of the River Senegal proper, but an isolated spot some twenty kilometres from Kayes. Again, the reports were of good fishing, and I had double-checked that it wasn't associated with human sacrifice, or anything out of the ordinary!

Ominously, a couple of hours before we set off, I began to feel odd. Nothing I could put my finger on, just a vague sense of unease. I can't remember, but I guess I put this down to memories of my experience at the waterfall. My father drove us to our destination, the last five kilometres along rutted tracks barely deserving of the description 'road'. By the time I arrived I was feeling really bad. 'Soul sickness' is as good a description as I can come up with; there were no physical complaints, but I felt a weight of oppression that was truly debilitating. I got out of the car with the others, but had no interest in fishing. We were at a section of the river that ran through an area of black igneous rock, and the black rocks made the water look dark and foreboding. After wondering around aimlessly for a few minutes I told my father I was feeling ill, and returned to the car to lie down. As I lay I felt as if the Gates of Hell had opened, and that I was being propelled toward them. There was a sense that I was facing existential annihilation, coupled with some sort of spiritual torture. Growing up in a Christian fundamentalist household, I interpreted all this as God speaking to me, warning me of what lay ahead if I didn't change my ways.

Well, I didn't get on my knees and repent. I began to feel better after we set off home, and by the time we got home I was fine. Still, the experience stayed with me, filed away at the time in my mental filing cabinet under 'Weird Shit That Happens To Me'. It has only been in recent years, and in the light of my occult explorations, that I have been able to make certain connections between such seemingly baffling occurrences and my magickal path.

As I began my study of Enochian magick, to be covered in my much more detail later, I discovered information concerning the 'Ninety-One Parts of the Earth', each ruled by a different Governor. I suppose as someone who was flung around the world at a dizzying rate when I was young, and who today lives in a country that is neither that of my birth nor nationality, geography is always going to be slightly more interesting to me than to many others, but I also found myself pondering the significance (if any) of my early travels, and wondered whether the Enochian system might be able to cast some light on this matter. My foreign travels seemed to be associated with spiritual experiences and lessons – could these be tied in any way to the Aethyrs (levels of spiritual experience) and Governors of Dee's magick?

Thinking about these experiences in Africa recently, I decided to figure out which Governor rules Mali. I soon discovered that 'Opmacas', Governor of the 7th Aethyr 'DEO' has jurisdiction over this country. I'm not suggesting that Opmacas was shadowing me during my time in West Africa, but in the light of the significance Enochian magick was to later have for me, it seemed reasonable to see if any connections could be made between the spiritual experiences I had whilst in Mali and the qualities of both the Governor and Aethyr associated with that country. A factor at the back of my mind whilst considering this was karmic links with place and country. Studies of people who claim to be able to remember a past life generally show that they are re-born into the same rough geographical area as the one they lived in during a previous incarnation, suggesting spirits can be drawn to places, and likewise that places have spirits.

Getting back to Opmacos, his 'tag line' is 'He who is from the beginning'. When I learned this it immediately struck me as interesting that Mali is the home of the Dogon people, whose ancestral myths seem to contain knowledge of Sirius B, a star that is not observable to the naked eye. According to such writers as Robert Temple, aliens visited the Dogon people 3,200 years ago, imparting this astronomical information. I think we can certainly conclude that whether the Dogon are 'from the beginning', the ancestral knowledge they have retained certainly is about as ancient as any extant.

In the case of Yemen, its Governor is 'Pocisni', of the 28th Aethyr 'BAG'. BAG is attributed to the element of fire, and Pocisni is said to be 'He who visits those in heaven'. We seem to have moved here from ideas of visitation from above to focus on Man's ascent skywards. Pocisni immediately made me think of the ancient stargazers from that part of the world who later came to be known at the Three Wise Men – and who certainly would have been in the habit of looking heavenwards! Interestingly, Yemen is a mountainous country, where many of the population are 'projected upwards' by virtue of the topography of the country. Furthermore, my father has often told me about the Yemeni obsession with building ever higher houses, and that there is a competitive element to this, whereby if a Yemeni's neighbour adds an extra storey to his house to overshadow surrounding buildings, this is often seen as an incentive to add an extra couple of floors to his own home.

So what could be the relevance of this to my own magickal path? It does seem that countries that I spent my formative years in have Governors that emphasise the earthward and skyward traffic of men and aliens (or angels). I'm not suggesting that I'm Enoch, and am about to 'walk with God', but I think this is significant given the central importance Enochian magick has come to have in my life, as demonstrated, amongst other things, by the very fact that I am writing this book.

CHAPTER FOUR

Soon after starting at University I decided that it was time to begin a proper exploration of the occult. At the back of my mind was the thought that it might all be a load of rubbish, but I figured the only way to find out for certain was to explore magick purposefully. The time felt right for a number of reasons. I was now living independently, and didn't have to worry about crucifix-bearing parents storming into my room mid-ritual. I was also at an age when the chaos of the first rush of adolescent testosterone was beginning to subside, and although I had my studies, there were plenty of free hours in the day.

Where does a seeker start? Fantasies of a cloaked guru waylaying me on Hampstead Heath didn't seem likely to become reality, so I started where I guess a lot of us begin: an occult bookstore. I was lucky in that, living in London, I at least had a lot of good stores to choose from. Though it's not a shop I would automatically make a beeline for nowadays, I think my first shopping spree was carried out in Mysteries, in Covent Garden. They now seem more interested in selling dolphin-shaped crystals with aura-warping properties, but back in the early 1990s it was primarily a bookshop. Wandering in one afternoon, I was overwhelmed by the number of different titles. I began to browse, all the while trying not to invade anyone's body space in case I inadvertently pissed of a witch, who I imagined would undoubtedly do some of her crazy witch shit on me. As a total novice, I imagined that anyone in an occult bookstore would be some kind of high adept, in town for a couple of days before they returned to their haunted castle in the Scottish highlands. I bought a handful of titles, amongst them 'Magical

States of Consciousness' by Dennings and Osborne and 'Psychic
Self Defense' by Dion Fortune (no point taking risks I figured)
plus some incense for good measure.

It was a couple of days later – a Saturday afternoon if I recall
correctly – that I decided to get down to business. I had decided
to try a pathworking from 'Magical States of Consciousness'. I
had read the book's introductory chapter, which sounded sane,
referencing psychological concepts I could relate to from my
readings of Freud and Jung. It seemed the book would provide a gentle introduction to mystical realms, with no danger of
having Beelzebub gatecrash proceedings. After a simple opening ritual, the pathworking involved simply reading a guided
visualisation that led one along the 32nd path of the Tree of Life,
from Malkuth to Yesod. This I duly did, and though I found
the imagery described quite potent, there were no spontaneous
visions, and I was certainly aware of my surroundings throughout the reading. At the end of the pathworking I felt slightly
deflated. I hadn't wanted to experience anything *too* strange,
but a little strangeness would have been good. Having overcome
my fear of 'dabbling with the occult' to do the pathworking, I
thought the very least the occult could do was show me it was
something to be dabbled with. I'm grinning now as I write this,
aware as I am of what lay just around the corner.

Later that day I attended a friend's birthday dinner at a nearby
Indian restaurant, and it was there that reality started to take
a turn for the strange. Halfway through the meal, whilst talking excitedly to the person opposite me, I happened to look
up at a large mirror hanging on the wall in front of me, which
was engraved with a depiction of the Hindu goddess Kali. The
second I saw her image it felt as if a switch had been turned on
somewhere in my brain. The fires of spiritual eternality cauter-
ized my mind, as, mouth hanging open, I was engulfed in a
wave of ineffable bliss. Words really can't do the experience
justice; suffice to say that it was the most powerful experience I
had ever had, and while it lasted I wished it would last forever.

I came to my senses to find the person I'd been speaking to
looking at me strangely. I apologised. I couldn't say how long

I'd been 'away', but obviously during that time she might as well have been talking to a statue. The normal noise of a busy restaurant now sounded deafening, and within half an hour I had made my excuses and left. I wanted to process what had happened on my own.

Later that night, things got stranger still. Standing in front of the mirror, brushing my teeth, I found myself staring into the reflection of my eyes. I guess I normally look at myself, if only briefly, while I'm having a brush, but for whatever reason, that night I found myself entranced by my own reflection. After two or three minutes of mirror gazing, I found my body getting progressively heavy, and my eyes seemed locked into their focus with an intensity I couldn't shake. Throughout this experience I think my sense of time altered, but after what seemed like fifteen or twenty minutes I began to slip into a very deep state of gnosis. I ceased to be the person I thought I was, and became aware (without getting any specifics) of a life (or series of lives) that stretched far back in time and would extend far into the future. This 'knowing' came with a huge sense of relief. Why should I care if I graduate with a good degree, get a good job, and find a good wife? 'I' was so much more than my present incarnation. The truth of these 'knowings' was unshakeable as I received them. I could not have been any surer about them if a scientist had presented me with a time machine, and given me the opportunity to travel forwards and backwards in time to meet the different versions of 'me' I was now aware of.

I was in a very comfortable state whilst these revelations were being received, but then my temples began to vibrate, at first mildly, then with some force. This feeling intensified, until it felt as if I was plugged into the mains. I began to think that my head was going to fall off my shoulders if the vibrations didn't subside. When they got unbearable I decided to break my gaze with my reflection. This proved hard! Like trying to wake yourself up from a dream, I had to use a combination of physical muscles and mental squirming to snap myself out of the trance. I succeeded in due course, but then suffered a sort of psychic blow-back. The vibrations stopped, to be replaced by an unpleasant prickling sensation all over my body. It literally felt like I was being jabbed by thousands of little pins simultaneously. More worrying was the sense of fear. Part of this stemmed from a suspicion that I might have gone mad. Was I having a schizophrenic episode here? The greater part of these feelings of terror, however, was directly linked to my 'knowings'. The shock of being exposed to an experience that is so outside of normal waking reality made me realise just how little I knew, how much was 'out there', and that the significance of this was enormous. I had opened a door onto a different reality, and even if it were shut, I could never lose the memory of what I had experienced.

As the prickling continued, my fear grew. Would I have to live with this for the rest of my life – lives? I cursed my occult meddling. I began to link what had just happened with my earlier pathworking. I grabbed my copy of 'Magical States of Consciousness' and began trying to burn it in my sink. After fire had consumed the first ten or so pages, and I was still feeling freaked and prickly, I decided to call my father. I was reluctant to ring him, feeling it was a concession of defeat in the disagreement we had long had over religion and God, but I was desperate. Mercifully, by the time I had got dressed to go out and find a payphone, the worst of the fear and prickling had subsided. I undressed and lay on my bed, wondering what the fuck had just happened.

What *had* just happened? There is no doubt in my mind that the pathworking I had done several hours before these events had been the trigger. The 32nd path represents spiritual awakening and the first steps away from the materiality of Malkuth. What I find interesting in the light of greater experience is the way this guided visualisation acted like a depth charge. The images and symbols the path comprises were seeded in my subconscious during the pathworking, and then later, when I was relaxing in a restaurant, they blossomed and gave me a vision of beauty, of the ineffable nature of spirituality. The mystical experience in the restaurant profoundly changed me, but also left me in an altered state of consciousness, which made me susceptible to the self-hypnosis that took place while I was brushing my teeth. Hypnosis is a very powerful tool – a truly magickal tool despite the associations we have with it today due to its popularity as a tool for curing phobias, and its use amongst entertainers as a way of getting quick laughs. The hypnotic state I inadvertently induced may have just led me to have a bizarre half hour in front of the mirror, had it not been for the events of earlier that day. With the earlier magickal working having seeded my mind, my hypnotised state lead quickly into a state of gnosis, which became so profound I began to experience energetic symptoms (the buzzing feeling) which were probably a precursor to astral projection. I may even have astrally projected briefly; there was so much going on during this episode that a brief exit from my body may have occurred without me being aware of it.

So, it took all of six hours to go from a sense of disappointment at my first magickal experiment, to being blown away at the vistas that could be glimpsed through the occult. From suspecting that I might be deluding myself in thinking magick was anything more than ritualised psychodrama, I was now reluctant to proceed further without the greatest caution. This was an important milestone for me. The supernatural had always seemed to have had a way of intruding on my life uninvited; I now knew that it could be *invited* to manifest quite successfully. In the light of subsequent practices, I can see that exploring the 32nd path of the Tree of Life is like taking the lid off a pressurised container. Our occult heritage from past incarnations (which is suggested by the very fact that we are exploring the supernatural in this life) lies dammed up whilst we are fully immersed in mundane life, but will burst forth as soon as it is given an opportunity.

The following day I slept in until about four o'clock in the afternoon. When I awoke I felt groggy, and not quite 'with it'. Over the following days my mood worsened, until I entered a state of depression (undiagnosed, but I suspect if I had sought a diagnosis it would have been confirmed). The symptoms were those many people are familiar with: general malaise, low energy levels, a tendency to sleep excessively, and an inability to concentrate. The very fact that I was depressed suppressed any urge I might otherwise have had to seek help or try and figure out why I was feeling the way I was. I guess I just thought it would blow over. And it did, after about three months. The end of this depressive period was heralded by an amazing dream. Most dreams are just a jumble of fragments of events from the previous few days, but this was one of those that shake you to the core. In it, a winged angel stood before me in a wood. He halted my progress with an upturned hand, and demanded I take my clothes off. I protested, mumbling something about wanting to preserve my modesty, but the angel insisted. I was ashamed of my garments as I removed them – they were tatty and smelly and I am pleased to say nothing like the sort of clothes I would normally wear. As my rags hit the ground they dissolved into the earth, an act that I found satisfying. I looked up, and saw that the angel was approaching me, holding in his hand a robe of brilliant whiteness. I took the robe, and pulled it over my head. The cloth was cool on my skin, and I immediately felt empowered and invigorated. The angel smiled at me, and said that my life was going to get better. The being took my hand and we walked for some distance until we reached a large clearing in the forest that bordered our path. I was led over to a large patch of white sand, in the middle of which was a black bowl that also contained sand. The angel picked this bowl up and handed it to me. I held it, noticing that the shallow bowl was made of black glass. The sand was fine – any finer and it would probably be better described as dust. The angel instructed me to find a similar vessel, which like the one I was holding had to be filled with sand, and this I was to keep at the foot of my bed on a permanent basis. I agreed to do this – any instruction the angel had made I'd have gone along with – and soon after the dream ended.

I felt much better when I awoke the next morning. I immediately remembered this dream, and within a few days had managed to find a saucer made of dark glass which I filled with sand bought from an art supply store. Placing the vessel at the foot of my bed one night for the first time, I was intrigued to find out what would happen to it whilst I slept. The next morning I checked, and the sand looked just as it had before I had gone to bed. It was the same story the next day, and the day after that. Thinking I had perhaps taken the dream a little too seriously, I forgot about the bowl. It remained at the foot of my bed, but I often failed to check it in the morning.

Pleased that I was feeling so much better, I put a lot of effort into my studies and spent some time patching up friendships that had been neglected during my depressed period. A friendship with a girl on my course turned into something more, and she, partying and my studies became the three things that occupied my time and thoughts. Then, probably three or four weeks after I had carried out the angel's instruction to fill a saucer with sand, I had another powerful dream. In it, I was skimming across the earth unaided at a terrific speed, passing numerous landscapes. Sometimes I was over water, other times land; I zipped across cities, villages, mountains and deserts, always at such a velocity that I barely had time to register the scenery below me before it changed. Then suddenly I was in a tunnel, now moving at what seemed an even greater speed. Ahead of me was a bright light. This light was so intense it was painful to look at, but at the same time I felt compelled to gaze at it. I would stare for a few seconds, then close my eyes when they started to hurt. When I looked at the light for the last time, I saw that a symbol had appeared on this globe of brilliance. I had just time to commit the symbol to memory, when the dream ended abruptly. The shape I had seen, as I remembered the second I woke up the next morning, resembled a hockey stick with an exaggeratedly curved end. It didn't mean anything to me, and I didn't give it much thought until later that day when, tidying my room, I had to move the sand saucer. Glancing at it, I saw that the sand had been disturbed. Looking closer, I could see that etched into the sand was exactly the same symbol I had seen in my dream! At first I wondered if an ant or small insect had crawled onto the medium. This seemed to be the only possible explanation for the strange impression, though even this wouldn't explain the coincidence of the symbol appearing both in my dream and in the sand. I could see no tracks, however, and as I looked more closely I could see that the symbol didn't look as if it had been made by insect legs. Its outline seemed to have been created by a precise collapse of the sand – the lines were even and smoothly defined.

I showed the sand to a couple of friends, without explaining the history of the saucer – I think I told them that it was used as an ashtray. They all admitted that the pattern was strange, but didn't seem overly excited by it. I think the most plausible explanation given was that there had been a pocket of air in the sand that had collapsed, leaving the impression of the symbol. This might indeed be what happened, but coinciding as it did with an identical dream image, I thought it significant. It was many years later, as I was delving into the magickal explorations of John Dee, that I realised just how significant the symbol was, being the Enochian letter 'Ged', which equates to our letter 'G'.

The dark patch I had experienced after my night of craziness, coupled with approaching exams, meant that for several months I deliberately stayed away from further pathworkings or other occult practices. I did start a daily practice of meditation, which, along with engendering greater calmness brought my nightly dreams alive dramatically. I continued to keep my bowl of sand handy – with some reluctance I had replaced the symbol-bearing sand with freshly sifted grain – but during this time there were no further shape appearances.

Just before my first year exams I was wandering around a shabby indoor market in Kentish Town. It had a similar feel to the covered sections of Camden Market, but being much smaller, and on a high road dominated by charity shops and bookmakers, it had a melancholy, lifeless feel to it. Most of the stalls were selling cheap clothes, but as I was wandering around, keeping an eye out for books, I noticed a sign advertising 'Mr Charles, Clairvoyant and Mystic'. I have always been sceptical of people plying their arts in such a way, suspecting their talents for taking money are greater than their talents at divining the future, so I deliberately avoided eye-contact with the man as I passed by his table.

'How are you today?' Mr Charles asked as I walked past.

Not wanting to be rude, I said, 'Fine,' but didn't slow down.

'Come on. Come over here,' the man said, beckoning me with a hand.

'I don't have any money,' I said firmly. 'I'm a student.'

'That's okay. No charge. Just take a seat.'

We sat looking at each other for a moment, before Mr Charles said, 'You're an old soul, that I can tell. What's your name?'

'Jon.'

You've been coming back to this earthly plane for a long time, Jon. Did you know that?'

I shook my head.

'One thing you're going to have to watch out for in life, Jon, is women who will try and fuck you for your power.'

At that stage in my life my concern was finding enough women to fuck, not being taken advantage of by the fairer sex, so this sounded way off the mark. I was also wary of being flattered as a prelude to being asked to pay for a full reading. It's fair to say that at this stage I was distinctively unimpressed with the man's words.

'You need to keep walking, Jon. Get that energy out, or it will consume you. In later life you're going to have to watch out for problems with mental illness and the law – you could get locked up in a hospital, or a prison.'

This didn't sound like flattery. My interest in what the man had to say increased.

'As I say, keep walking. Talking of walking, your sister may have some trouble with her leg soon. Maybe an accident. Could be worth ringing her and asking her to be careful.'

We spoke for a few minutes more, before I left, thanking the man for his words of advice. Couple of interesting things about what he had to say. Firstly, about two days later my sister was hit by a car whilst crossing the road. She didn't sustain life-threatening injuries, but did break her leg! Secondly, as later chapters will show, the words of warning given to me proved to be quite accurate. A couple of years ago I saw Mr Charles again, this time in Camden Market itself. We made eye contact as I passed his stall, but it took me a few seconds to realise who the man I'd just seen was, by which time the Sunday afternoon throng had carried me away. I almost went back and paid for a reading. Something, maybe a fear of what else he might have to say, stopped me.

After my first year exams were over I managed to get my hands on some acid for the first time. I'd been wanting to try LSD for ages, but the nearest I'd come to acquiring any up to this point was being sold some untreated paper in Leicester Square (yes, I should have known better). When I finally got hold of the real thing I started in style, taking a full black micro-dot. With me were two more experienced trippers, Big Paul and Little Paul, fellow students at the LSE. We were still in halls of residence at the time, having two weeks between the end of exams and when we had to vacate.

We dropped our tabs at about five in the afternoon, and over the next few hours went through the (now) familiar stages of waiting, feelings of euphoria, and being off our heads. The three of us were gathered in Little Paul's small room, and I distinctly remember looking out the window at the night sky and being sure that the room had somehow become detached from the building it was contained in and been hurled into space. With The Orb playing in the background, the setting was just about perfect for some inner space exploration.

As the night progressed I found I couldn't leave mirrors alone, and spent some time staring into one as the two Pauls talked. I seemed to see a wolf's head as I looked at my reflection. This image felt quite comfortable, as if I was staring at something that represented part of my atavistic heritage. We wandered out of the room at one point, into the flat's communal area. I can't remember what we were trying to do, but five minutes after we returned there was a knock on the door – it seemed that one of us had thrown a lit joint in another flat resident's open suitcase. She was not very happy with us.

Later on we left the flat to go and explore the strange planet our spacecraft had landed on. We 'bounced' down Gainsford Street, through Tower Bridge Piazza (marvelling at the huge stone people sitting on benches who didn't seem to want to talk to us) and then on to Tower Bridge itself. Back then on the southern bank of the Thames there was a small park to one side of the bridge, and here we lay on our backs and stared up at the night sky. Pretty soon geometrical patterns started to super-impose themselves on the blackness. I was amazed at the detail they displayed – they weren't just blobs of light, but intricate, fluted, spoked designs. One pattern that stuck in my mind was of several concentric circles with what resembled clock hands – lots of them – that whirled around, first clockwise, then anti-clockwise. The shapes seemed to have intelligence, or be the creation of something that possessed it. Toward the end of our time in the park I felt a sudden stillness descend. A mist seemed to rise from the river Thames, and in it I saw what looked like angelic beings, tumbling with each other as they sought to grasp a golden crown that one of them had dropped.

CHAPTER FIVE

After University I began training as a Chartered Accountant. I think in choosing this job I was giving reign to a hitherto undetected masochistic streak, for it was surely one of the worst decisions I have ever made. As someone with no huge enthusiasm for mathematics, and who has never enjoyed detail at the best of times, I couldn't really have been more unsuited to this career. I made a good fist of it for a couple of years – not by showing promise as an accountant but, in the words of one of the partners, 'helping company morale'. This I achieved by my drunken antics when I was away on audit, and generally giving off a stoned vibe (which often was because I *was* stoned).

Two years was enough for me. I bailed before getting my piece of paper, and whilst I don't like failing to complete something I've started, I like being driven crazy even less. I wasn't just leaving to do nothing, either. I had a little money I wanted to put into a property business, I wished to spend more time growing a rare book business, I had a book to write . . . and I wanted to do magick!

The buying and selling of rare books was something I had been doing since I was an undergraduate. A pretty middle-aged pursuit for someone of eighteen, but I've always had a deep connection with the written word. Thoth is a god that has a special place in my heart and mind. I served an apprenticeship without master of six months of sometimes costly mistakes, but had gradually become proficient at finding first editions at low prices which I could sell on at a nice profit.

The worlds of magick and books started to mingle soon after I left accountancy. Sometimes I would wake up in the morning, take the underground to whichever station 'felt right', then, after getting off, literally let my legs carry me where they would. It's a strange sensation, detaching your legs from your mind. Especially in big cities like London, your feet tend to just be tools for rushing with, getting from A to B in the least possible time, and so to allow them the freedom to guide their customary master is weird. They had a job of sorts – to guide me to books – but how they did that was up to them. Often I would find myself wandering down what looked like incredibly unpromising roads – rough, nasty streets where the locals don't read, and the only shops are off-licences and launderettes – only to turn a corner and find a little charity shop with a treasure trove of books inside. This method of 'shamanic walking' led me to a tiny auction house tucked away on an industrial estate in Leyton. At its weekly sales I was typically the only one bidding seriously for books, with the result that I could often pick up several boxes for less than a fiver. The books I bought there often reflected the local area – I once ended up walking away with thirty brand new copies of an anthology of Reggie Kray's poems (titles such as '20 Years In Jail' and 'I Was A Hooker') – but there were some real finds that cropped up on a regular basis. I noticed that if I was reading a book by a particular author I would often find a collectible title by the same person the following week at this particular auction house. I went so far as to sometimes intentionally buy and read a paperback by an author whose works I wanted to find, and two times out of three this worked.

Half way through my first year of self-employment I began having lucid dreams. I used the popular technique of looking at your hands throughout the day, at the same time asking yourself 'Am I awake?' as the means of triggering them. As anyone who has had a lucid dream will testify, it's so liberating to realise mid-dream that you are dreaming, and then be able to explore your environment without the limitations of waking-life physics.

One of the first lucid dreams I had involved me examining what looked like a microfiche reader, or computer screen, with pages of text scrolling upwards at a high speed. It was hard for me to catch any of the text, but I did see the words 'Moon Child' at one point. Surprise, surprise then, when the following day, hunting for books at a local antiques fair, I came across a first edition of Aleister Crowley's 'Moon Child', being sold at a price that showed the owner had no idea of its value! This is the closest I have come to an experience that approximates a viewing of the Akashic records, and I find it quite apt that the information I gleaned related to the written word.

Just before Christmas 1995, I had a lucid dream that I will never forget, and which has taken on much more significance since my Enochian explorations began in earnest. I woke up in a dream, to find that two strong men were holding me by the arms. Their grip was tight, and I had no doubt that I was being detained. I asked what was happening, and a disembodied voice from above me said, 'You're being taken to meet your selves.' Before I had time to ask what this meant, the men holding me began to march me at speed along the tunnel I could now see we were standing in. The tunnel slopped downwards, and after what seemed like a mile of walking we came to some stairs that led downwards. I resisted descending these, but was forced to take them by the men holding me. Down, down we went, then along another tunnel, this one smaller than the first so that I had to stoop to avoid scraping my head against its roof. Finally we came to an archway, where we paused for a second before I was flung into the room on the other side. I fell to my knees, and when I looked up I saw a woman – slim, dark, with large breasts and wearing a short skirt, high-heels and a revealing top – sitting on a stool. I tried to talk to the woman – to ask who she was and what she wanted – but my mouth couldn't form the words. But then, I didn't really need to ask her, as I knew who she was – she was me! A man walked up to the woman from the blackness behind her – he was slight and looked quite effeminate – and stood beside her. This man didn't say anything either, but again, I knew he was me. After this, more and more people walked from the darkness to stand beside the other two. They came in different shapes and sizes, in a variety of different attires, and were young and old, black, white and every shade in between. Moreover, they were all me! I stood before them flabbergasted, thinking to myself that I need never feel lonely again. Suddenly, from above the throng, a white screen appeared, about the same size as you'd expect to find in a movie theatre. It remained white for about a minute, then I saw the countdown you often see at the start of an old newsreel – the numbers nine to one appearing, each digit contained within a circle. There followed jerky black and white footage of a man ascending a number of steps to what looked like an altar of some sort. He waved his arms melodramatically, after which there was a puff of smoke, and an angel appeared. On seeing this being the robed man retreated some way down the stairs, then bowed, and generally did a good impression of grovelling. The angel looked on with a serene expression on its face, then, with an elegance of movement, signalled to the man to approach. The man walked back up the stairs until the two were almost facing, at which point the angel lifted its hands to adopt a pose reminiscent of an orchestral conductor about to begin his directions. Instead of launching into a frenzy of stick waving, the angel lifted its right arms upwards. The man looked in the direction the angel was pointing, and simultaneously the scene changed, to show a grid about twenty rows wide and twenty rows deep, each containing letters. My first thought on seeing this display was that it was some sort of periodic table. I knew enough about chemistry to know what a periodic table looked like, without knowing enough to realise that this was not one – or not one that would be recognised by a scientist. Later chapters will show that my first impression was not entirely crazy.

As I continued to watch the grid, I saw that adjoining squares were being highlighted together – both boxes would become noticeably brighter than all the others – and then the two would merge, 'spawning' a third letter, which would then fall from the grid like a scrabble piece that had been dropped. The two squares that had been involved in this process would then return to their original state for a second, before the last box in this duo would flash bright with the next square along, and again a merging and spawning would commence. As an avid scrabble player I watched all this with curiosity, but remained confused as to what, if anything, it might mean. Luckily I was keeping a magickal journal at the time, so these details were recorded for later review.

It was around this time that I made one of my most interesting book finds. I received a call from a woman living in Dagenham, in response to a newspaper advert I was running at the time, offering cash for books. Her brother had recently died, and she was keen to get rid of the many books his flat contained. Without meaning to cause offence to any of its inhabitants, Dagenham isn't a part of the world I would normally associate with fabulous books, but the woman kept stressing the man's eccentric and scholarly interests, so I thought it unlikely I'd have to sift through piles of books about football and the Second World War.

When I turned up at the property the following day I was met outside the building by a woman in her early Sixties. She led me to the flat entrance, and opened up. I hate resorting to talking about 'strange atmospheres' or 'weird vibes' but this flat had both in abundance. Walking into the home, I felt a heaviness and despondency that was almost physically tangible. I knew immediately that the woman's brother had committed suicide, something she confirmed without prompting a little later.

As well as having a loathsome feel to the place, the flat was a junk heap. What furniture it had was largely obscured under piles of newspaper, there were clothes strewn everywhere, and in the hallway was what looked like a disassembled wardrobe. Against almost every free section of wall were piled stacks of books, and I quickly noticed that they were indeed the sort of titles I could sell on easily. There were lots of scholarly history and archaeology books, plus a fair few occult titles.

The woman was obviously embarrassed at the state of her brother's flat. 'He just never got it together, poor lad,' she explained. 'Plenty of brains, but he was a dreamer, and could never apply himself to anything.'

We quickly agreed on the price – the woman didn't want a fortune, provided I agreed to take all the books. This was a common request when on such visits – people are often more interested in clearing a house than realising a huge sum for the books they have. I returned the following day with a hired van and in two trips had carted away all the man's books. Then began the process of sorting through them all. This began with an initial cull of books I wouldn't have a use for – these I typically donated to charity – which reduced the stock by about a third. Then I began to divide the remaining books into two categories – run-of-the-mill books and those that would fetch higher prices and would need more care in pricing. The Internet was just beginning to offer a means of selling books, but valuable titles would generally go to specialist dealers or be sold at auction.

It was during this second sorting of the books that I came across the diary. It was unremarkable to look at – a cheap A5 book with ruled pages – and I very nearly tossed it without even opening it. I'm glad I didn't. Opening it up, I saw a tiny, spidery handwriting filling the pages, and began to read. I felt guilty at reading a dead man's most private thoughts, but not guilty enough to stop. The author might have been glad his words had found an audience, I told myself. The first entry I looked at, dated some three years earlier, wasn't particularly gripping, describing a meeting the deceased man had had with his older brother. The author obviously resented his sibling's success and 'normality', which he had twisted in his own mind to represent some sort of crippling conformity. I thought about the state of the dead man's flat, and decided that 'conformity' certainly had its advantages.

Flipping on a couple of pages I came to an entry that began 'Invocation of the Lesser Angel ACCA from the Air Tablet . . .' My interest spiked immediately. The guy had been a book man *and* a magician. I read on, but couldn't understand much of what followed – it was all about keys and angles and angels. Then there was a description of some sort of vision or waking dream, which was vividly described, involving a crisp, fallen leaf that was carried up by the wind to the upper atmosphere, where it was pummelled by winds before being sucked into a cloud, whereupon water droplets had condensed on it, causing the leaf to fall back to the ground. It landed in a wheat field, which had been harvested apart from a section of crop that formed a large T-shape. There followed the man's analysis of the vision, complete with a description of the chemical processes behind the decay of vegetal matter, and the substances that can be leached out from them by rainwater. There was also the use by the author of the word 'Enochian'. I had come across the term in books I had read, but at that stage knew next to nothing about it. In my mind it sounded Biblical and somewhat uninteresting. Little did I know. . . .

Around this time I did a magickal working, based loosely on a ritual outlined by a prominent chaos magician, the object of which was to bring me a valuable book. The working incorporated concepts from physics, in particular the idea of parallel universes – ideas that I wasn't familiar with at the time, but which have become much more important to me in recent years. My clearly expressed desire was to find a book worth in excess of £5,000 within one year of the ritual date. I was tempted to 'request' a book by a particular author, but decided that that really would be a huge ask.

The ritual was performed, and duly forgotten about. Several months passed, until one day I found myself walking down Upper Street, Islington. As I neared the tube station I saw in the distance that someone was selling second hand books from a table on the pavement. As I got closer, I saw that one of the books had the distinctive yellow dustjackets that Gollancz have published a lot of their books with. Getting nearer, I saw that it was a copy of John Le Carre's 'Call For The Dead'. I knew this was his first book, and that if it happened to be a first edition it would be worth a lot of money. My heart was thumping as I picked the book up and saw that it was indeed the first edition. Not just that, but it was in great condition, and had been priced up at a mere twenty pounds!

I reached for my wallet, and would you believe it, it was empty! I'll confess that the thought *did* occur to me that I should just walk off with the book, but instead I put it back down, covered it with a couple of other titles, and went off in search of a cashpoint. The gods were really tormenting me that day. The first cashpoint I found had a queue about twelve people long, and the next one was out of order. Eventually I found a machine that was working and wasn't being used, and withdrew cash. By this time I was some way from the bookstall, so I jogged back. Nearing my target, I panicked when I saw someone holding the book I wanted to buy. I walked straight up to this person – a man in his forties – and started to blabber on about needing to buy this book for my father. It was only then that I realised I was talking to the stall owner – I thought another customer had picked the book up! The man had obviously seen *me* pick the title up, and was giving it a closer inspection.

'I'm selling this way too cheaply,' the man said. 'I could probably get forty quid for this down the West End . . .'

'I'll pay that,' I said, far too eagerly. 'My father loves Le Carre. He'd be so happy if I got this for him.'

The bookseller waved the book in front of my face teasingly for a few moments, then relented and said, 'Go on. It's yours.'

The man placed the book in my sweaty hands, I gave him two pieces of paper with the Queen's head on it, and off I went. At the time I estimated the book to be worth around five hundred pounds. A little research later that day suggested its value was nearer three thousand pounds, and I eventually sold it for four grand!

At this time I was living with my then partner Sarah. Sarah had been to a Tarot reader once, but that was the extent of her experience of the paranormal. To begin with she viewed my growing interest in the occult with bemusement, not really sure whether this was a passing phase, or something more important. I think a lot of 'normal' people think that being into magick is the by-product of reading too many fantasy novels, a sort of Dungeons and Dragons game where the line between fact and fiction has become so blurred that the participant has forgotten he or she is just playing a game.

Toward the end of this first year of self-employment, my daily practices were beginning to move some strange energies in me and the house, and Sarah started to have alternate realities intrude on her day-to-day existence. Poor girl! One afternoon Sarah announced that she couldn't find her watch, an expensive Tag Heur. As someone who slept, showered and swam with her timepiece, this was an almost impossible occurrence. She remembered looking at it at just after eleven o'clock in the morning, but at three it wasn't on her wrist. I had no idea where the watch was, and to be honest didn't give it much thought. Then later that evening as we were both sitting on the sofa watching TV, Sarah suddenly shrieked and picked up an earring from her lap. It had just fallen off. She checked the other ear, and the earring that should have been there was missing as well. It was at this point that I started to wonder if something other than forgetfulness was at work, a notion that strengthened when we both noticed that a ring Sarah had worn from the age of fifteen – a treasured gift from her Grandmother – was missing as well! We both got up and started searching for the watch and ring – our goal being as much the ruling out of weirdness as ensuring they were safe. We turned the house upside down, but couldn't find any of these items. My sense of strangeness was amplified by the fact that coinciding with these events I kept seeing balls of pink light on the periphery of my vision. I had seen them before, over the preceding couple of weeks, and had understood them to be thought forms that I had lost control of (I had done some work to create such thought forms, but they were meant to only appear when I made a gesture with my left hand). Were these simple astral entities to blame for Sarah's missing jewellery? My thoughts were interrupted by yet another shriek. I ran down the stairs to where Sarah was, and she informed me that the earrings that had earlier dropped off, and which she had reattached to her lobes, had fallen off yet again!

What was happening here? My personal opinion is that the thought forms I had created were attacking my partner! This episode coincided with a tense period in our relationship, and in fact it was soon after this that we broke up. It would appear to me that the thought forms I had brought into existence had evolved a degree of autonomy beyond that which they were meant to have. Nevertheless, as my creations, their activity seemed to be directed toward expressing my feelings. Of course, I didn't consciously want them to strip Sarah of her jewellery, but this may have been the easiest way in which they could express the animosity I was feeling toward her at the time. I find it interesting that my stray thought forms had an 'interest' in metallic objects. Entities are often trapped in rings and other objects of jewellery – is there something about metals that they feel an affinity toward? In later chapters we will see that there may be something about the intrinsic properties of the elements that is of significance to occult practices.

Returning briefly to the danger of uncontrolled thought-forms, two further examples spring to mind. Both involve men of about my age, one a former work colleague, and the other the friend of my partner. For reasons that aren't that relevant, I developed an obsessive hatred for both guys. This wasn't a half-hearted dislike; we're talking a full-on, all consuming, so-strong-it-almost-hurts, detestation. I would spend long periods of time imagining the most awful injuries befalling these people, visual-izing limbs being wrenched from their bodies and blood gushing copiously. And that, in my view, sealed their fates. Just as a bit of back-story, around this time, whilst in a state of meditation, I would sometimes try to influence pieces of electrical equipment in my house. It was an unscientific PK experiment, made easier by the fact that I was living in a rented, fully-furnished, dwelling. My normal target was the microwave, and most commonly I would just visualise the led display breaking – just going blank. I would emerge from the bedroom after finishing my meditation expecting to see that the microwave had packed up, but it never had. Then one day I had a particularly extreme confrontation with the guy from work I hated. On the tube on the way home that night I must have spent a good fifteen minutes imagining him receiving the most appalling beating. In my fantasy he only remained alive to be able to see what a mess his attacker had made of his body. The commute went quicker than normal, and when I got home, would you believe it, I noticed the microwave led had stopped working! The machine would heat food, but the timer/clock display never worked again. You had to press buttons and hope for the best when using it. I felt I had achieved a partial success in my PK experiment. I saw the earlier visualisation I had been doing as having laid the ground-work – released a spore of possibility if you like – which the state of gnosis I had gone into during my hatefest earlier on the tube had activated. But there's more. This all happened on a Friday; on the Monday when I went into work I discovered that the colleague who was the focus of my hatred had been attacked and hospitalised over the weekend. Returning to his car on the Saturday after a night out, he had been beset by two attackers who beat him to within a couple of blows of death. We didn't see him for about a month – that was how long the physical wounds took to recover – and when he came back it was obvious that the mental scars would stay for a long while longer. Coincidence? Maybe, but the occurrence of the micro-wave breakage on the same night as my detailed imagining of a fate very similar to the one that befell my colleague makes me doubt this. Both were acts of negative visualisation that I think fruited at about the same time.

Nor was this the only time something like this happened. About ten years later I found myself boiling with hatred toward an old friend of my partner Liz, a guy called Mick. The origins of these feelings were mundane and childish, as is so often the case, but this didn't take the edge off how I felt. We saw each other from time to time at social gatherings, and it was at one such an event that we nearly came to blows. We were both totally drunk, which made matters worse, and though we stopped short of trading blows I said to him at one point, 'I'll get you killed, you know.' I didn't hire a hit man the next day – I was ill in bed with a hangover – and it was a couple of years later I next saw Mick. We encountered each other in the street, not at a party, and although we didn't speak it reminded me of the threats I had once made. I remember thinking, 'You're still alive!'. Two weeks later Mick was dead. He had been at a huge bankers' Christmas bash held in the grounds of the Tower of London, and toward the end of the night had walked up a long flight of stone steps. Somehow he had managed to fall over, and ended up with a brain haemorrhage that put him in a coma. He died two days later without regaining consciousness. Coincidence? Maybe, but I'm very careful who I hate these days.

I was seeing a lot of Paul at this time – he of my Glastonbury evocation experience described in Chapter One. Paul was very interested in the occult, with a special enthusiasm for the Qabala. His approach was more cerebral than mine – he found the concepts of Hermetic thought appealing, but didn't seem as keen on getting 'stuck in' to spiritual practices as I was. Paul was a guy with problems. He was well educated and had a good job, but years of substance abuse were starting to take its toll on him. I sensed an underlying depression that stemmed from his childhood experiences, and this was being exacerbated by the vast quantities of pills and pot he was consuming.

One evening he came over to my place, and brought with him a couple of tabs of acid. I hadn't had any LSD for three or four years, and wasn't particularly keen to indulge further. Nevertheless, in the spirit of comradeship, I agreed to half a tab. We dropped at about six in the evening, and things duly became non-Euclidean and fluid. It was quite a gentle ride for me – the half dose, and the fact that it wasn't a very strong batch combining to ensure that though unmistakeably altered, I was very much in control of myself. We talked outrageously for a few hours, then decided to go for a night stroll. The house I was living in at the time backed onto woods, and we headed for these. The night was warm, the stars bright, and it was great to be in a natural setting, even allowing for the occasional branch that caught us in the head as we walked. We eventually found a fallen tree near a small stream, and sat on this for an hour or so, just listening to the sound of the running water and talking. Up to this point, it was the gentlest and most peaceful trip I'd ever experienced.

We got back to the house just before daybreak, and it was at this point that Paul's mood changed drastically. From being immersed in his trip but happy, he switched to speechless melancholy. His expression 'collapsed', as if the muscles in his face could no longer support the mask he had been wearing. He sat speechless, hunched forward, and even began to rock gently like someone suffering from autism.

'Are you okay, Paul?' I asked.

He didn't reply, and just stared through me as if I was not present.

I waited a few minutes, hoping this strange mood would pass, before asking again, 'Are you okay?'

Still no reply.

I found my hand moving toward the cigarette lighter lying on the table in front of me. Without knowing why I was doing it, I began to trace banishing pentagrams in the air with the lighter's flame. In the darkness, and with the help of the LSD, the pentagram seemed to hover between Paul and I for several seconds after the flame was extinguished. I traced the same pentagram again, and again asked, this time with more urgency, 'Paul, *are* you okay? Come on, snap out of it!'

This time I at least got a flinch out of him – he could obviously hear my words. I looked straight into Paul's face. Suddenly the visage I was familiar with disappeared, to be replaced by a face of total hideousnes. The face made your typical medieval gargoyle look angelic in comparison. So horrible was it that I felt fear, but I also sensed that whatever I was looking at was a manifestation of the problems besetting my friend. In as real a sense as you're likely to get in such matters, I believe I was seeing the entity that possessed him.

I continued to gaze into Paul's face, and the demon continued to stare back at me. I was repulsed, but also intrigued. This was a glimpse of one of the denizens of hell that few people ever get. Remembering the lighter, I decided to give this ghoul a good dose of pentagram magick. I again made a banishing pentagram in the air, inches from Paul's face. The spirit didn't like this. No, not one bit. It was like shining light on a vampire. The gruesome face seemed to contract in on itself. Multiple mouths that sat concentrically seemed to start eating each other and other parts of Paul's face. This sight was so disgusting I felt like throwing up. I couldn't take much more of this entity, but decided the best solution was to get rid of it. I again flamed a pentagram, and this time imagined it floating into the horrible face. Paul grimaced when this was done, but it was Paul grimacing, not the spirit! Suddenly my friend seemed to be back with me. His face now looked much softer, as if it had undergone extensive age-reversal.

'Paul, how are you feeling?' I said.

He blinked, as if waking up from a deep sleep, then said, 'A bit strange. Why were you flashing that lighter around?'

'I don't know. You seemed to go a bit weird.'

'I felt a bit weird. I feel . . . I feel like crying now.'

This statement made me feel uncomfortable. Our conversations had always been about ideas, never emotions. Still, I preferred an emotional Paul to a possessed Paul. I could see he was fighting back tears. I suppose I should have said 'Do you want to talk about it?' and brought out the tissues, but I was a typical bloke and announced that I was going to make some tea. We didn't talk about what had happened. We watched the Simpsons. Let me tell you, the Simpsons are the best antidote to the powers of darkness. . .

Since that evening, I have often wondered how large a part the LSD played, both in creating Paul's strange turn of mood, and in my perception of his 'demon'. The conclusion I have come to is that the drug just amplified something that was already there, but in no way created the scenario. Whether Paul's demon had a name or not, or really looked like the grim entity I saw, its appearance to me was real in the sense that I was given a glimpse of the shadow that seemed to stalk him. The hideous form it had I believe was its astral form, a glimpse of which I was able to get with the help LSD. As Jung said, very often a belief in spirits is the simplest and most straight forward way of understanding whatever 'it' is that seems to behave in the way they do. A psychologist might describe Paul's demon as a 'cluster of emotional problems stemming from abuse suffered in early childhood', but that wouldn't explain why this 'cluster of problems' reacted so adversely to a pentagram.

A couple of months after this, Paul and I went on a 'pilgrimage' to Stonehenge. Or at any rate we drove to Salisbury, checked into a hotel, and then tried to get into Stonehenge after darkness had fallen. 'Pilgrimage' sounds a lot more impressive, however. There were a couple of problems with our plans – most notably that you can't actually get any closer to Stonehenge than the fence that surrounds it. Our troubles started as soon as we jumped into the car to make the drive to the famous monument. We were both very stoned after a spliff in our hotel room, and struggled to navigate our way out of town. We drove around in circles for about twenty minutes, before staggering into a petrol station and asking the sales assistant how to get to the site. She told us, but by the time we had returned to the car we had forgotten her directions. Cue another twenty minutes of driving around the streets of Salisbury, before unknowingly returning to the same petrol station. It was only after I had opened my mouth to ask for directions that I realised that I had spoken to the same person some minutes before. Her look as she repeated herself made it clear she thought we were crazy hippies, but I guess they're probably used to them in Salisbury.

More through luck than anything we finally got to Stonehenge and parked up. We had totally underestimated how substantial the fence around the monument was, and how far from the stones it is, making night-time appreciation of the site limited. This didn't faze Paul, who quickly decided to try and climb the fence. He'd barely touched the wire before a guard came over, and asked what we were doing. 'Trying to get in,' Paul said, with admirable honesty.

'Well, you can't,' the guard said. 'Restricted access.'

'How so?'

'Just the way it is.'

'As a British citizen I have the right to spend some time with the stones,' Paul said. 'Open up.'

The guard was about to reply, when we all heard a squeak.

'What's that noise?' the guard wanted to know.

'Just my hamster. I brought a hamster with me.'

I was aware of the hamster – Paul had said he was going to bring it with us on our trip and release it ceremonially at the ring of megaliths – but didn't think he had actually done so.

So there we were, the two of us and a hamster, trying to nego-tiate access to Stonehenge at 11 o'clock on a Saturday evening. The only thing missing was a druid to really complete the night for us. Needless to say, neither Paul, myself, nor the hamster were allowed in, so we had to settle for circling the perimeter fence for ten minutes, with Paul occasionally shouting 'Nazi!' at the guard.

After we had finished admiring what we could see of the stones, Paul insisted on releasing his hamster. I tried to explain that the hamster might struggle to survive without a human to feed it, but Paul was adamant that it had to be freed, and that it would thrive on the magickal energies of the place. Finding a suitable spot some distance from the monument, Paul took the hamster from his pocket and placed it on the ground. He mumbled some words that I couldn't catch, then whisked his hands away flam-boyantly. The hamster remained still, obviously bemused by what was happening. 'Go!' Paul instructed loudly. The hamster might have twitched its nose, but it made no attempt to escape. 'Go!' Paul commanded, even more loudly. Still nothing. Paul spent a further five minutes ordering the hamster to flee, but the creature was having none of it. Eventually we had to admit defeat, and I persuaded Paul that we should bring the animal back with us.

When we got back to our hotel we chatted for a bit, had another spliff, then decided to try a psychic experiment we had first played around with in Glastonbury. Taking the Major Arcana cards from a Tarot pack, Paul would shuffle these then cut the pack. My challenge was to try to determine which card lay on the top. My technique, known by names such as scrying, travelling in the spirit vision, and remote viewing, was to close my eyes, clear my mind and wait for images to arise. For whatever reason, that night I was hugely successful in this task. Sometimes when attempting to do this, I would be tanta-lised by images that had to be decoded before they led me to the card in question. As an example, I might get an image of the Vatican, which would make me think of priests and popes, which in turn would lead me to guess 'The Hierophant' as the target card. This night, however, it was effortless and direct. In seven out of the nine attempts I made, I got a flashed image in my mind's eye of the card in question, complete and detailed. It's a weird phenomenon to describe, but if you can imagine looking at something just as a camera flash illuminates it, that is the nearest I can get to explaining how it feels. The beauty of these 'flashes' are that they are unmistakeable and not open to subjective interpretation. I see the card, and that's all there is to it. With the foggy glimpses I sometimes get, the images received can often be associated with a large number of cards. An image of a woman, for example, could be said to relate to The Empress, Temperance, Justice, The Star and The High Priestess.

There is something awe-inspiring about experiencing an unmistakeably psychic experience. A queue of scientists, psychologists and rationalists a mile long could each spend an hour with me explaining to me why what I have experienced is self-delusion, a mental aberration, wishful thinking, luck, etc. and I would laugh in their faces. Paul became quite alarmed at my success that night – it seemed there wasn't anything I couldn't tune into – and it was interesting to see the last shreds of any scepticism he may have had about my abilities give way.

Such psychic successes would, during my Enochian explorations, become crucial to me. I would be using a very similar skill to communicate with the angels, and knowing that my abilities were real would be very important to me as I grappled with the significance of the information I was getting.

CHAPTER SIX

Towards the end of my first year of self-employment I met Gerry through a mutual friend. Gerry is an author who has published a number of titles on the Tarot. When I met him he was running a Tarot School from his home in North London, and he soon persuaded me to take his Tarot course at a reduced rate. I wasn't that interested in learning the art of card divination, but was drawn to Gerry personally, who has a magnetic personality. Also, I'm ashamed to confess that I was excited by rumours that many of Gerry's students were nubile young women, and that cards might not be the only things being spread at the Tarot School!

On arriving for my first Tarot lesson, I was met at the door by a turban-and-cloak-wearing Gerry, who bowed expansively as he welcomed me in. His Tarot School was housed in a large room on the ground floor of his house, which had been decorated with plaster pillars, steles, tribal masks, and Egyptian deities, so that it looked like a storage room for out-of-favour museum pieces. I was suitably impressed, and became more impressed when he mentioned during this first lesson that there were other 'courses' available to those who had completed the Tarot lessons.

Whilst the Tarot course comprised primarily of one-to-ones, there were weekly 'socials' at which I got to meet other students – who *were* primarily female. Gerry also had an interesting concept of New Age networking, whereby he would send his students past and present off to various parts of the country to meet other New Agers, most of whom he knew but hadn't been students of his. This was fun, and with time on my hands I would drive off at weekends to hang out with Siberian shamans in Brighton and Celtic silversmiths in Cornwall.

One such individual I hooked up with was 'Lucy Buffalo', who was inspired by the Native American tradition, and worked as a healer. She was in her late forties when I met her – old enough to have taken part in an orgy with Rod Stewart in the Seventies, as she once let slip.

I went to visit her at her cottage in Derbyshire, and within ten minutes of arriving it became apparent that we would become friends. Her healing work involved the transmission of subtle energy – call it chi, prana, gimblets – whatever you like, and I will never forget the first time she gave me a demonstration of her abilities. Sitting some three metres from her, she directed her energies at me, and within seconds I was shaking uncontrollably. It felt like my core body temperature had dropped by about ten degrees. I found her ability to manipulate my physical body fascinating – such a powerful demonstration of the existence of unseen forces. I once arranged for her to meet a particularly sceptical friend of mine, and it was hilarious to ask him what he made of her skills while they were being demonstrated on him. He couldn't answer, because his teeth were chattering so violently! He went away from his meeting with her a very confused materialist!

As I got to know Gerry more, I found him a fascinating mixture of opposites. He was an adept teacher, with some well-developed psychic skills. He was also an adept con-man, and once showed me a tiny pencil that is clipped on to the end of a fingernail, used in card readings to make the client think that angels have been scribbling messages on the Tarot deck. He was a spiritual idealist, and at the same time a money-grabbing crook who 'borrowed' a five-figure sum from an elderly client – money she never saw again. These contradictions in the man made him fascinating, frustrating, and in the end very enlightening. I came to see the conflict his disparate selves created as part of the reason for his drive to achieve, but also a key contributor to his downfall, which I will describe shortly. One of the lessons I had to learn in dealing with Gerry was that his character faults did not negate the value of his skills or teaching. As I later read about other famous spiritual teachers and pioneers – Carlos Castaneda, Aleister Crowley and Edward Kelly, I was able to temper my assessment of their shortcomings with the experience I gained through knowing Gerry.

Soon after graduating, Gerry had spent about ten years travelling, moving east via Greece and Turkey to finally end up in Afghanistan. In Greece he had been imprisoned for a year for stealing from tourists. It was in Greece that he had first discovered the Tarot, and he had had a legitimate source of income there from doing readings for fellow travellers. Soon after arriving in Afghanistan he had developed an opium addiction, and it had been out of a need to fund this habit that he had been sucked into drug smuggling, acting as a facilitator for some of the Westerners who came to the country to buy for export. A tip-off that he was under surveillance by the C.I.A. and liable to be arrested shortly had led to him returning to the U.K.. The Afghanistan drug trade's loss turned out to be the London New Age scene's gain.

After my Tarot course completion ceremony, attended by eight or nine other students plus a host of freaks and friends, Gerry decided that we should all go to Hampstead Heath, where he wanted to perform a public evocation of a god . . . whose name I can't recall. We duly piled into cars, and arrived at the Heath at around ten o'clock in the evening. We found what we thought was an isolated spot, and Gerry soon got down to the business at hand. I should mention that Gerry was in his Eastern Prince garb – flowing robes and headdress. I also recall that he had a large wooden staff. A couple of students were holding huge candlesticks, fitted with cylindrical glass wind-breaks to enable them to be used outdoors. Gerry was in the middle of calling upon whichever deity he wished would visit with us that evening, when we were puzzled to see the headlights of a vehicle heading toward us. Thinking a passing motorist had strayed from the nearby road – and alarmed at how this could have happened – we turned to watch as it neared us. The car was heading straight for us, but as it got nearer we could see that it

was a park warden's vehicle. No sweat – we weren't commit-
ting a crime – but I at least was embarrassed. There were two
wardens in the car, which pulled up right next to our circle.

'Can I ask what you guys are doing?' one of the men said.

'As free citizens, we are exercising our right to perform to
perform a simple religious ceremony,' was Gerry's reply.

I don't think the warden knew what to say to this. There are
bye-laws to cover most sorts of nuisance activities that can
take place in parks, but I don't think there's one prohibiting
evoca-tion ceremonies.

'Well mind you don't start lighting fires,' the warden at
the wheel said, referring to the candles, before the pair drove
away.

Gerry had a very interesting personal morality, or anti-
morality as it would be better described. His starting point was
that notions of 'right' and 'wrong' were meaningless – there was
no such thing as a universally acceptable code of conduct, and
that what people thought of as such was just a consensus-view
that served the purpose of preventing anarchy. As far as Gerry
was concerned anarchy was a good thing, though he reserved
the right to clobber anyone that threatened him physically or
financially. In everyday life Gerry liked to adopt the concept of
being a 'person-state', who decided what was or wasn't appropriate for the sole citizen of this nation – himself. In cases where
he was tempted to commit what according to the laws of the
United Kingdom would be classed as a crime, the act was seen
instead by Gerry as a disagreement between two states.

'But what if everyone declared themselves a person-state?' I
remember asking Gerry on one occasion. 'There are sixty million
people in the U.K.'

'To qualify as such they would have to have the realisation
that they *can* see themselves in this way. That takes care of 99.9
percent of the population, who wouldn't. Of the tiny number
who have the insight, all but me and two or three others have
the balls to act on it. There are plenty of criminals, but they're
mainly just chaotic idiots. They should do themselves a favour
and indulge in a bit of activity re-classification. In international

affairs everything boils down to power. If a powerful nation invades a small country and occupies it – especially if it is populated by black people – it is called colonisation. If a powerful country occupies a relatively powerful country populated by whites – think Germany and France – then it's an illegal invasion. They're the same act, but one is 'wrong' and one is 'right'. In the same way, if my state commits a crime against the state of the United Kingdom, but I have the 'power' to get away with it, then as far as I'm concerned it is 'right'.

I must have looked unimpressed, because he went on: 'What's a law, apart from a bunch of people getting together and agreeing that something should be illegal? And who are these people? In this country they're individuals that have been voted for by the moron masses!'

'You don't think there are universal ideas of goodness?' I asked. 'Karma? You don't buy into it?'

'A fox eats a chicken,' Gerry responded. 'Is it wrong to do so, or is it just hungry and doing what comes naturally?'

'Yes, but humans have more intelligence than foxes,' I said. 'A fox wouldn't be able to understand the difference between right and wrong.'

'What does understanding right and wrong have to do with it? An act is surely right or wrong – if you accept such concepts – whether right or wrong is understood or not. If a mentally handicapped person kills someone else, is it not murder because he doesn't understand what he's done?'

'That's why the law distinguishes between murder and manslaughter,' I said.

'So the intention is more important than the act committed?'

'In a way.'

'Would you rather be killed unintentionally or have someone intentionally try and kill you but fail?'

'The latter, but in such a case it isn't my morality or karma in question. From the point of view of this other person his con-science would be easier in the first case.'

'Really? You'd feel better having accidentally killed someone than you would if you'd failed in an attempt to murder?'

I had to think about this one.

'If there were universal concepts of 'goodness' and 'badness', then these would surely be evident in nature and the animal kingdom,' Gerry continued. 'But that isn't the case. Take destruction. If I went into someone's house and spray-painted all over their walls, I would be considered to have broken several laws. I broke into a house, I committed criminal damage, etc., etc.. But what about a volcano that erupts and spews lava down for miles around, destroying many acres of beautiful forest and killing hundreds of animals and insects. How are the two occurrences any different?'

'There was no malice in the case of the volcano eruption,' I said. 'Plus with the volcano eruption there is at least the creation of fertile soil that comes from the outpouring of lava, so in years to come a new forest will grow back that is even healthier than the old one.'

'I might not have any malice in breaking into someone's house. I might just want to do it, without wishing the owner ill. And by ruining his house's interior decor you could say that I'm giving him the chance to redecorate. He might have had horrible decor, and my 'crime' might enable him to decorate tastefully.'

The conversation began to become quite disturbing at this point, and I soon changed the subject. It was a topic we returned to on several occasions, however. And thinking of myself as a state in dispute with the United Kingdom *has* made the odd bit of law-breaking easier to deal with.

Okay, so do you want to hear about how Gerry went mad? I thought so. I met Gerry near the peak of his short-lived success. Soon after I made his acquaintance a married Lebanese businesswoman, who had come to him for a Tarot reading, accused Gerry of rape. No-one apart from Gerry and this woman will ever know what really happened. I suspect Gerry was innocent of this charge, and that his client simply saw a rape allegation as a way of dealing with the feelings of shame that arose after their encounter, but I can't be sure. Whether guilty or not, two months after I met him, Gerry was arrested, charged and bailed, pending trial.

Gerry tried to cope with the stress of his predicament by turning to drugs. His drug of choice was speed, his addiction escalating rapidly to the point where he was injecting it. He was also taking Estrogen tablets, 'so that he could experience what it was like to think like a woman'. I remember thinking he should have started his course of female hormones a couple of months before he met his accuser, as it might have saved him and her a lot of suffering. His fascination with the female psyche tied in with an interest in cross-dressing, which I was vaguely aware of.

The combination of his intake of near-lethal quantities of speed, and the Estrogen supplements, resulted in a sharp decline in his mental condition. He quickly moved from being a bit weird and slightly jittery to a more or less permanent psychotic state. Gerry was married, with a young daughter, and both wife and daughter soon moved out. Pretty soon I was getting disturbing late-night telephone calls. In one, he informed me that the C.I.A. had planted spies under his floorboards. He'd ripped a few up to try and find them, and though unsuccessful he was sure that he would catch them soon enough. In another call, he claimed that he'd discovered that his wife was the head of an international paedophile ring, and that her departure from the family home was an attempt to evade arrest.

Everyone that Gerry knew or came into contact with was written into a bizarre script that saw the man as the victim of a universal plot to persecute him. (I later learned that I was at the time suspected of being a police officer who had been ordered to befriend him in the hope of obtaining evidence against him in his rape charge – this despite the fact that I met him before the allegation was made.) Jack, a Tarot student who was also lodging with Gerry, was accused of being the reincarnation of a man whom the latter had murdered in a past life. His mission in this lifetime was to avenge his death at Gerry's hands. This sounded insane to me, and you can understand how baffled and scared Jack felt when Gerry challenged him about this.

'I'm moving out,' he told me, after relating Gerry's theory to me. 'I'll need a week to find somewhere else, but I'm going. The guy is nuts.'

I would have offered to put him up at my place, but it was just too small. 'I think you'd be wise to go,' I said. 'Just try and keep out of his way until you do.'

The next time I spoke to Jack, two days later, he was standing on my doorstep.

'Sorry, mate. I tried to call but your phone was switched off. I just had to get out of there.'

I glanced at the rucksack that lay on the ground beside him, before beckoning him in. 'So what happened?' I asked as we walked through to the living room.

'Gerry has been cleared of his rape charge, but he's worse than ever. I was just watching the telly, when a brick came through the living room window. Then Gerry poked his head in and asked if he could come in for a coffee. The fucking weirdo was wearing nothing but ladies knickers and a bra.'

'Fucking hell.'

'I just told him to piss off, then ran upstairs and grabbed a few clothes and left. Can I stay the night here?'

We spent some time discussing what to do next. It was apparent that Gerry was becoming a danger to himself and others, but the police weren't likely to be interested in an act of vandalism committed against his own property.

'He needs be sectioned,' I said.

'How do we arrange for that to happen?' Jack asked.

'I don't know,' I said. 'I'll ring my G.P. tomorrow morning. He'll probably be able to advise on getting him examined.'

In the end the police got to him before the shrinks. A phone call the following morning from Gerry's wife informed us that after Jack had fled, Gerry had knocked out all the glass in the living room window, entered, and then proceeded to demolish all the furniture in the room. He'd then jumped into his car, still dressed in just knickers and bra, and driven off.

It was about eight months later that I next heard from Gerry. He had just been released from Cardiff prison.

Incarceration had got him off the drugs, and he sounded quite normal as he related the events of his last night of liberty. After pulling off in his car, he had headed west, eventually ending up on the M4. Somehow, as he was nearing Cardiff, he had found himself driving on the wrong side of the motorway. He was pulled over by the police before he could cause an accident, his arresting officer no doubt surprised to find Gerry attired in women's undergarments. A search of his car was made, and Gerry's supply of speed was found.

'It was fucking mad when I got pulled. I thought I was in role-playing game. I was Bilbo Baggins, and I was pissed off that my captors were dressed in police uniforms. You know, cops and robbers is a different game. They'd walked onto the wrong set. They were trying to handcuff me, and I was telling them to piss off, calling for Gandalf.'

'So how long did you get?'

'Six months. Dangerous driving and possession of a controlled substance. I represented myself in court. Didn't really matter what was said, or who said it, I was going down anyway. I had a bit of fun though. Tried a style that was part Martin Luther King and part Oscar Wilde. There were a few laughs, but I was found guilty and sentenced.'

Prison didn't faze Gerry much. He'd done time in worse places. He took up Buddhist chanting while locked up, beginning his recitations at five in the morning. He related that the chanting used to set some of the prisoners off, so that they started shouting demonically. The implication was that they were being affected metaphysically, but I suppose another possibility was that they just didn't appreciate being woken up at that time of the morning.

I didn't stay in touch with Gerry for long after his release from prison, as he soon moved to Ireland, where he briefly re-invented himself as a Celtic shaman. Recently, however, I discovered that he has just been released from prison (yet again). This latest stint was far tougher than his time at HMP Cardiff, involving three years at the notorious Glendairy Prison in Barbados, his crime this time trying to smuggle cocaine. Now approaching fifty, I hope he confines his criminal behaviour to fare-dodging in future.

CHAPTER SEVEN

My relationship with the nuts and bolts of physical existence – eating, sleeping, supporting myself – has been always been a difficult one, swinging between extremes. After a period of intense spiritual seeking and experimentation during my first year of self-employment, the pendulum swung the other way, and I found myself being tempted by the god Mammon. Actually, he wasn't so much tempting me, as enslaving me. One of the self-employed activities I was involved in was small-scale property development, and, as I began to acquire properties, I found that they each had voracious appetites as far as my financial reserves were concerned. Buying property to rent out was meant to free me from financial concerns, but in the short term it did just the opposite, making me sweat over invoices. My budding property portfolio was a long term play, and whilst in recent years it has started to give back, in the early days it deprived me of the profits I was making from my book dealing, which had to be funnelled into keeping my empire afloat.

After the purchase of my second flat, I decided to get a job as an estate agent. There were a few reasons for this decision. Firstly, when you're pyramiding – using the rise in value of your properties to finance further purchases – there is invariably some waiting involved for capital appreciation to occur. The house market had sprung into life after a deep decline, but even the shrewdest of buys don't appreciate 20% overnight, meaning I had time to kill while I waited for gains to accrue. Secondly, though I had enjoyed my escape from accountancy and its associated terrors, I was feeling a bit isolated. Spending the whole day on your own is okay for a while, but I'm sufficiently sociable to find indefinite solitude depressing. Thirdly, I needed the money. My flats weren't paying for themselves, let alone paying for me.

I will readily confess to having reservations about this decision. Like most of the population, I viewed estate agents as gel-haired monkeys. I felt deserving of a more rarefied work milieu. Nevertheless, I needed to earn money, meet people and keep in touch with the property market. There wasn't really an alternative.

Landing a job in estate agency was an interesting process, as it involved the reverse of most people's tricks for gaining employment. Instead of tarting up my C.V., I dumbed it down. 'A's at A level became 'C's, etc. The question on application forms 'Have you been convicted of any criminal offence in the last five years?' I soon learned had to be answered in the positive rather than the negative.

I was eventually taken on by a small firm, and assigned the role of 'lettings negotiator' at their Wapping office. Given the limited vocabulary of most estate agents, I've always found the term 'negotiator' perplexing when used to describe the spivs that populate this profession. 'Negotiator' makes me think of the U.N., hostage crises, and stuff like that – not the mobile-clutching, loud-tie-wearing, braying individuals that like to work in property.

As an introduction to my new working environment, let me introduce some of the characters I found myself sharing an office with. There was Marcus, the lettings manager, who drove a top-of-the-range Mercedes, at the expense of eating or paying bills. When I joined he was embroiled in an unfair dismissal case, having fired a female employee whose job description had turned out (to her surprise) to be quite . . . broad. There was Phil, a Neolithic throwback, who didn't so much sell flats as intimidate people into purchasing them. He had frequent leaves of absence from the office – time spent consulting with his lawyers about a forthcoming rape case. We had Jessica, who couldn't understand why any of the banker clients she screwed on their first date didn't want a second date. Michael, the office manager, was an Essex Epicurean with a bowel obsession. If he wasn't gushing about the amazing meal he'd enjoyed the previous evening, he was giving us a plop-by-plop account of his most recent visit to the toilet.

Into this Moron Soup I was flung, and, after my previous comments, you'll be surprised to learn that I actually enjoyed swimming around in it for a while. I did a course in anthropology at university, and it was through the eyes of an anthropologist that I experienced my new environment. Everyday, new insights were gleaned into the strange 'tribe' I had joined. 'No' meant 'yes', I soon discovered, and vice-versa. Their holy book was the office diary, which was consulted on an hourly basis to determine what clan members were meant to being doing at any given moment. The diary contained details of appointments made, with each member of staff being assigned a different biro colour, so as not to overload limited brains as any given page was perused. Each entry consisted of an applicant's name, their contact number, which properties were to be viewed, and either the abbreviation C.I.T.O. (Coming In To Office) or M.A.P. (Meet At Property). I often considered making a diary entry for one of my co-workers (in the appropriate colour) along the lines of '2pm. [Colleagues name] [Their home address] [Their telephone number] [Have long think about career choice.] M.A.P..

I spent two and a half years working in estate agency before finally leaving the industry. The first six months in the business grounded me substantially and was a good experience. I was rescued from the fairies and forced to confront the realities of hard brick and hard money. Not to diminish the value of the year that preceded my time in the property industry, but I still had lessons to learn in terms of balancing the mystical with the mundane. Unfortunately, I was eventually sucked into the materialistic mind-set of the estate agency business. Flats bought at knock-down prices through the company I worked for made me richer, I found myself meeting attractive woman who didn't care that I had a partner, and one morning I did a double-take as I found myself climbing into a brand new BMW to drive to work. Who had I become? The pendulum, it seemed, had swung totally the other way. Balance! Why was this lesson proving so difficult to learn?

The truth always outs, and self-destructive behaviour is one of the plainest indications that all is not right with an individual. Occasionally, sitting in the pub with a friend after work, I would notice that the first pint of beer was gulped down, with an urgency that had nothing to do with normal thirst. I remember having the thought on one such occasion, 'Am I turning into an alcoholic?' I used to dismiss such suspicions as soon as they arose, but it turned out that my instincts were spot-on.

My drinking stayed at 'heavy partier' levels for another few months after my first worries surfaced, but then the combination of the end of my first marriage, coupled with the stress of a move back into full-time self-employment, seemed to tip that delicate balance into full-on alcohol dependency. I can actually remember the day this switch occurred. I had had a late night out with friends, and in the early afternoon of the following day, it suddenly occurred to me that I wanted a drink. Not only that, but I was going to have one, all on my own, and with nothing to celebrate apart from the fact that there was a full bottle of Jack Daniels in the cupboard. I helped myself to a first generous measure, then a second, a third . . . and before I knew it, I was having my very own party. My new girlfriend (the reason behind my marriage break-up) arrived back from shopping at around five o'clock, but I said nothing about the whiskey I had drunk, and was able to act relatively normally. Lying about drinking came very easily to me.

Although I know now that this particular day signalled a move from heavy to alcoholic drinking, I was of course unaware of this at the time. I think I just thought I was being a bit crazy with the lone, daytime consumption of booze that had begun at this point. And of course, I was still functioning. If you caught me on any of the three or four days in an average week when I didn't drink, you would never have guessed that I had developed a problem. It is, however, an unfortunate fact about alcoholism that it is progressive, and once you 'have it' you never return to normal drinking. The only way to ensure you don't end up seriously damaging your health is to stop drinking completely. As one of the guys I know from Alcoholics Anonymous says, an alcoholic can point at those in a much worse position than him or her – those that have lost families and jobs, those who have been incarcerated, those who need a liver transplant – and say, 'We'll I'm not *that* bad,' but the truth is that they are only 'not that bad *yet*'. As certain as the daily rising of the sun is that if an alcoholic continues to drink, sooner or later he or she will lose his mind, body and possessions. The progress of the disease is inexorable and relentless; nothing but death or abstinence will stop it ravaging its sufferer.

Over time my binges became worse and worse. There would normally be a couple of days in a week when I didn't consume alcohol, but when I was on it I was on it. I turned up to the birth of my son drunk, I pissed in phone boxes in the middle of the day, I emptied port bottles from friends' drinks cabinets on the sly, then topped them up with water. Jesus turned the water into wine; I turned the wine into water! Cocaine helped fuel these binges, allowing me to carry on drinking long after I would otherwise have passed out.

Without doubt the worst thing about my habit were the times when I was having one of my frequent 'mini-dry-outs'. As the anaesthetic that alcohol is was leached from my body I would start to feel the knocks I'd taken during my bender, the memories of the stupid things I'd done would return, and a cloud of depression would descend over me. In such states I could barely walk or talk. I would normally just sit on a sofa, watching television without really taking any of it in, and wonder how things could have gone so badly wrong.

I would often suffer from insomnia as I was drying out, even after days of getting very little sleep. I would lie in bed at night, craving a decent seven hours of unconsciousness, but being cruelly denied this respite from my aching body and general sense of self-loathing. Because I was so fatigued, even though normal sleep was elusive, I would often find myself in a strange mental state which, although not something I appreciated at the time, was a wonderfully altered state of consciousness. With my eyes closed, I would slip into waking dreams very easily. I was so tired that my rational mind did not have the energy to exercise its normal iron grip on my perceptions, whilst the insomnia caused by drying-out meant that I didn't tip over into normal sleep. When people ask me for advice on scrying, I am sometimes half-tempted to reply, 'Go on a three week bender, then stop drinking suddenly.' Certainly an experience very similar to spontaneous scrying is something I often experienced in such situations, and it's just a pity that I wasn't in a fit state of mind to put this opportunity to good use. I remember on a number of occasions seeing visions that were not far off the clarity of normal waking consciousness; it was the sort of 'movie' experience people sometimes wrongly think ordinary scrying always involves.

Often these visions would take a sinister tone. I would see demonic faces glaring at me as I lay in bed with closed eyes. Other times the imagery would be highly erotic – writhing masses of naked bodies in caverns bathed in a reddish light would be a typical sight. C.W. Leadbeater has described particular parts of the astral plane as being populated by the spirits of deceased alcoholics, and I have often wondered whether in having such experiences I was getting a glimpse of this zone. On one occasion I had the sense that the ghouls that surrounded me in my astral vision were those of drunks, and I even heard one of them saying, 'You'll be joining us soon!' I tend to believe that Leadbeater may be right in his comments.

My struggle with alcoholism is one that will last my lifetime, but the disease had complete mastery over me for five horrible years. Because I wasn't drinking every day, or homeless, or behaving in many of the ways people normally associate with a drinking problem, I found denial to be a bigger issue than many other alcoholics do. Additionally, I generally remembered little of my binges as I was often in a state of blackout or asleep whilst they were going on, so I had impaired memories of my worst behaviour, allowing me to conveniently 'forget' that this bad behaviour had happened. However I tried to explain away my problem, it was very real. At my worst I would lose up to a straight month to booze. This would be thirty days in which I had only fragmented and hazy memories of what happened; a month during which I might lose track of how many times I had been admitted to rehab; a month in which I might see the inside of an ambulance three or four times.

In recent years I have often thought about the words of Mr Charles, the Camden market psychic, who warned me all those years ago about detainment in a psychiatric hospital or prison. The former prediction came true, (via stints in rehab) and the latter prediction almost came to pass due to a drink driving charge where I narrowly avoided a custodial sentence. In the case of one my rehab stints, I felt as if I had been imprisoned. Having been admitted in the late afternoon, by seven o'clock in the evening I was beginning to feel the first effects of withdrawal, and a huge cloud of depression descended as fleeting memories of the chaos of the previous couple of weeks returned. I knew the sensible thing to do was ride it out, but the urge to drink and blot everything out was too strong. I went down to reception and asked to be buzzed out, on the pretext of desperately needing cigarettes. The receptionist was no mug, and said she would call for a nurse who could accompany me to the shop. Ignoring her suggestion, I returned to my room and paced for half an hour or so, before going back down to reception. I was considering waiting for the door to be buzzed open to allow someone else in or out, and then just making a run for it. The good news was that the person on reception had changed, and hence was unaware of my desire to escape; the bad news was that there didn't seem to be any traffic in or out of the building at that time. Even in my drink-addled state I knew I couldn't hesitate. I walked straight up to the receptionist, and indicated toward the door. 'Can I help you?' I was asked. 'Yes, I'm Dr Markson,' I said. Bear in mind that 'Dr Markson' had three days of beard growth, red eyes, and looked like he'd been sleeping in a sewer recently. There was a moment of hesitation – I could see she thought I was a strange-looking member of the medical profession – but such is the power of the word 'doctor' in a hospital, the door was buzzed open for me, and I left. I believe there was a delay of about fifty three seconds between stepping outside and having a beer in my hand.

There is a very obvious connection between alcohol and magick. Beyond the multiple meanings of the word 'spirit', there is the 'otherness' that both can allow individuals to experience. Additionally, in my case, having been brought up by evangelical Christians, there was a primitive and damaged side of me that saw my alcoholism as God's punishment for my 'dabbling' in occult matters.

Having reached a stage in my life where the urge to drink is one I can control I would have to say that overall I am very pleased that I developed my drinking problem. This may sound like a strange comment to make, and I can hear the shouts of dismay from the poor friends and family members who had to endure me at my worst, but let me explain. In my opinion, there is nothing quite like a severe addiction to test an individual to the utmost on every level imaginable. The addiction engages one physically, emotionally, intellectually and spiritually. Recovery from an addiction involves the individual working on each of these levels – and therein lies the challenge, and, if successful, the triumph, of overcoming the affliction.

What are the reasons for some people succumbing to alcoholism (or any other addiction) and others resisting? Doctors today believe genetic predisposition can make certain people more likely to become alcoholics – this explains why Celts, for example, have a much greater incidence of alcoholism, even allowing for other factors. Stress and social deprivation can also play their part – being driven to drink does quite literally happen for some people. Emotional and psychological disorders can be significant in contributing to the development of a drinking problem, also; borderline personality disorders, attention deficit disorders, anxiety-inducing neurosis – these are often present in alcoholics. My own view is that an often overlooked factor in alcoholism and many other addictions is the spiritual battle that is likely to be raging in the person affected. Alcoholics Anonymous seem to have an intuitive grasp of this fact, highlighting as they do the spiritual growth necessary in overcoming a booze

68 SPIRITS WALK WITH ME

problem. My own personal view is that past life spiritual experiences often create a tension in an individual; they are aware at a very deep level of the need to continue learning and growing spiritually, but resist this impulse because of the necessary pain this often entails. If the individual is not able to confront this choice in an open and honest way, the result I believe is often a 'dis-ease' such as alcoholism. I recall talking to a Christian psychiatrist, who believed anorexics and alcoholics – anyone with a mental illness – were possessed with a demon, and that occasionally she could catch sight of this demon, or perhaps glean its name. This highly educated woman could reconcile these apparently primitive beliefs with her clinical training; she was able to use both the accepted psychiatric model and a fundamentalist Christian faith when assessing her patients. Whilst I think the idea that everyone with a drinking problem is 'possessed' is a little simplistic, I think this approach to the problem does have some merits, and in some cases may be as accurate a description of what is happening as anything suggested by modern science. The psychiatrist that oversaw my own admission to rehab on several occasions used the word 'demon' when talking with me. He would often say, 'You have a demon inside you, and you can't forget this for one second. It will never go away.' I find the supernal triad of the Tree of Life a useful model for the understanding of addiction. If we take Kether as representing the newly born child, we can see that at this level of development (in fact, up until the age of 6 months or so) he is unaware that he has an existence separate from his mother – there is no sense of ego or 'other'. Chokmah represents the discovery by the child that he is an autonomous human being – he discovers 'me' and 'you'. With the discovery of a 'me' the child is for the first time confronted with the possibility of a past (life) and a future (destiny), and it is at this point that the first stirrings of a rebellion against his fate may occur. There has been a splitting from the One, which causes considerable anxiety, and if this process is not properly handled the third point in this triangle manifests later in life as a pathological merging with the darker aspects of Binah's watery nature. Instead of finding a sea of possibilities in this third Sephirah, a sea of illusion is swum in, aided by wine or other mind-altering substances.

I certainly don't think it's an accident that many artists and sensitives develop alcohol (and other substance abuse) problems. R.D. Laing made the assertion that schizophrenia was in many ways a natural reaction to the contradictions and craziness of modern life, and you could argue that alcoholics are taking a similar stance, opting out of consensual reality with a bottle of whiskey. Sitting in a traffic jam, trying to rush to an appointment that you shouldn't have to attend, listening to the news on the radio announce that the food you thought is healthy is actually killing you, baking in the car because your city lost its ozone layer five years ago, it is easy to see why being permanently sozzled is a fairly logical response to living on our planet as human beings.

A final word on alcohol and magick. When I first joined the Ordo Templi Orientis, I kept the fact from my then partner – I didn't want her thinking I'd joined a cult. If I was attending one of their meetings I used to say I was going to an A.A. meeting – which, given the longstanding association of the A.A. (Argentium Astrum) and the O.T.O., was almost true!

CHAPTER EIGHT

So now we come to the meat of the book, the Enochian revelations I have received, and the results of the research I have done to try and further understand the angelic magick of John Dee. My reasons for building slowly to this point are two-fold. Firstly, I think the spiritual experiences I had prior to immersing myself in Enochian magick contributed significantly to my becoming involved in it in the first place – you could even say that the angels came looking for me, and that I was in touch with them long before I'd heard about Dee, Kelly and The Great Table. As I write this I am reminded of the episode I had with the sand tray at university, where the shape that appeared one morning was that of a letter of the Enochian alphabet, and also the discovery of the diary that included references to Enochian magick in the house of the dead man whose books I bought. Secondly, I think an honest relation of real magickal experiences is very important to those who are involved or interested in the occult, and one of the goals of this book is to show that beyond arcane symbols and impenetrable theories, there is a world of mind-and-soul-stuff that can be experienced dynamically by the practitioner. It's very real and totally imaginary, and just wait-ing to be experienced.

Let's start with a brief account of the life of John Dee and his assistant Edward Kelly. We need to fit this duo into their historical and psychological context. John Dee was by all accounts a genius, a child prodigy who went on to explore such diverse fields as mathematics, astrology and navigational techniques. Ever loyal to Queen Elizabeth, he spied for her in Continental Europe, and was in fact the original '007', having adopted this glyph as his personal signature. (These three numerals look somewhat like a man shading his eyes with a hand, a pose a spy might well adopt in an attempt to conceal his identity.) Perhaps his single most significant trait was his desire to discover – whether this be advances in mathematics, the future (via his astrological work), the actions of foreign powers, the secret of the transmutation of lead into gold or . . . the Mind of God. Enter stage right Edward Kelly, a man who although intelligent in his own right, lacked Dee's all-round brilliance. While he may not have come up to Dee's standards intellectually, he possessed the gift of seership – in other words he had natural talents as a clairvoyant, and these, as we will see, were crucial to Dee in his attempts to penetrate the spirit world. Dee's left-brain emphasis needed the input of the right-brain Kelly to produce the results they did. While Dee was motivated by intellectual curiosity above all else, Kelly seems to have had monetary gain and physical comforts as his overriding drivers. Kelly is often cast as a charlatan, and it is true that trickery may have been one of his tools for realising his ambitions. However, as my dealing with Gerry the Tarot teacher taught me, just because someone cheats in one respect, that does not mean that they are obliged to cheat in all respects. Those with clairvoyant and mediumistic ability tend to be more creative than the average person, and so you could even argue that psychic ability comes with a tendency for its possessor to be elastic with the truth.

Dee and Kelly met in 1582, Kelly having been introduced to Dee by a mutual friend. Kelly's initial interest in working with Dee was the prospect it offered of allowing him to decipher an alchemical manuscript in his possession known as the Book of Dunstan, which he believed would allow him to make a red powder essential for the transmutation of base metals into gold. For Dee's part, Kelly, as a gifted scryer, presented him with the opportunity to communicate with the spirits he believed were trying to get his attention. By the time Dee and Kelly met, Dee had already worked with other psychics, but they were either not sufficiently gifted, or had prematurely terminated the working relationship. Almost a year to the day before Kelly's arrival, Dee heard unexplained knockings and voices in his house, and these strange occurrences had continued intermittently thereafter, prompting his search for someone who could help him converse with the entities responsible for these noises.

Sceptics looking for evidence that Kelly might have faked the results of his clairvoyant interaction with the spirits to prolong his time with Dee have pointed out that in addition to the possibility of alchemical breakthroughs that an association with Dee might provide, Kelly also benefited from a generous allowance paid by the older man. I think it is certainly possible that Kelly may have decided at the beginning of their relationship that he would fabricate messages if he needed to . . . but also very likely that in the end this became unnecessary as he was overwhelmed by the flow of detailed information he received from the angels.

Dee and Kelly's relationship lasted six years, during which time they travelled extensively in Europe, swapped wives . . . and spoke to angels. Their most productive period from a magickal point of view was toward the end of their association, especially a particularly intense stretch of around ninety days, during which much of the material we now recognise as the basis of Enochian magick was transmitted via Kelly. Dee maintained a pious Christian attitude to his magickal explorations throughout. Despite the persecution he faced at certain points for his occult interests, in his own mind he was simply a seeker looking for knowledge and guidance from the angels that God himself had created. His contacts with the spirits were proceeded by periods of fasting, contemplation and ritual cleansing, all designed to elevate his mind and spirit, and make himself a worthy recipient of the messages that were imparted.

The procedure Dee and Kelly used for their scrying sessions developed over time. To begin with, Kelly would simply kneel on the floor in front of Dee's desk and peer into a scrying crystal. The stone would be placed in a simple 'frame', a drawing of which can be found in one of Dee's manuscripts dating from December 1581. Kelly would pray aloud, calling on the target angel to appear in the crystal, whilst Dee would be in an adjoining room, likewise entreating the angel to show itself to his partner. Early on in their sessions the angels gave further explicit instructions on the apparatus that should be employed by the pair. These consisted, amongst other paraphernalia, of the scrying stone, the seven Ensigns of Creation (each associated with a different planet), the Table of Practice, the Sigillum dei Aemeth, and four lesser sigils, similar but smaller to the Sigillum dei Aemeth, which were to be placed under the legs of the Table of Practice. Once introduced, these items continued to be used for the rest of the pair's scrying career.

On the 14th of March, 1582, Dee and Kelly were shown by vision the design of the Ring of Solomon, an adornment of which the Angel Michael said, 'Without this ring thou shalt do nothing.' On April the 28th of the same year Dee was given his 'principle stone' by the angels. Looking up from Dee's desk during a scrying session, Kelly noticed a bright stone lying on a nearby mat. Previously unseen by either man, this was a gift from the angels, who told Kelly, 'Go toward it and take it up.' The stone fit neatly in the palm of a man's hand, and instantly became Dee's most prized possession, to be used thereafter as the men's primary scrying tool. In due course Dee received from Uriel the design of a personal magickal symbol of authority, or Lamen, which was to replace one supposedly given to him by an imposter posing as Uriel during Dee and Kelly's first scrying session. How Dee was to tell the real Uriel from the imposter Uriel we can only guess, but the 'true' Lamen certainly appears more authentic. Whereas the original design looks Goetic, the second version was composed of eighty-four Enochian letters, inscribed upon a square tilted so it rests upon one of its corners, bounded on four sides by a square that is oriented at forty-five degrees to the inner shape.

After the 'furniture' of angelic communication had been taken care of, the transmission of magickal instruction began. The first packet of information was the system of magick contained in the Heptarchia Mystica. As the manuscript of this work remained undiscovered when Casaubon wrote his 'A True And

Faithful Relation Of What Passed For Many Years Between Dr
John Dee and Many Spirits' – one of the primary sources of
information on Dee and Kelley's work – the Heptarchia Mystica
was for a long time neglected by Enochian scholars. Neither the
Golden Dawn nor Aleister Crowley ever make reference to it,
for example.

The starting point for the revelation of the Heptarchia
Mystica was the receipt of seven squares, each containing forty-
nine further squares. Every cell had a letter and number written
in it. From this primary source the Tabula Angelorum Bonorum
was extracted, which was a circle containing seven rings which
was divided into seven equal segments. All the information
from the original tables was contained in the Tabula Angelorum
Bonorum. Each segment, or sphere, of the Tabula Angelorum is
ruled by one of seven kings, under each of which there is a single
Prince and Five Nobles, giving a total of forty-nine angels. Each
Prince further governs a group of forty-two Ministers, who rule
in six cohorts of seven Ministers, each one ministering over
four hours (so that together a full twenty-four hours is presided
over). The general procedure for the invocation of the Kings
of the Tabula Angelorum Bonorum was to arrange the temple
furniture in the prescribed order (this would include a circu-
lar table of the forty-two Ministers who serve the day of the
ritual, laid on the floor, and on which the magician stands),
and to then address the Heptarchical King whose audience is
sought. Communication was effected through the scrying crystal.

On the 6th of May, 1583, the angels communicated to Dee and
Kelly details of the Enochian alphabet, which consists of twenty-
one letters. The characters of this angelic script are in the most
part totally unlike those in the English alphabet, with the
exception of Ceph, Na, Tal and Or, which look somewhat
similar to the English letters 'P', 'M', 'E' and 'F' respectively.
Some linguists who have studied the language of Enochian state
that it has its own grammar and syntax, making it unlikely that
it was easily concocted by either Dee or Kelly. Dee, one guesses,
could have attempted to create his own language, but not Kelly,
and certainly not in a short period of time.

It was not until April, May and June of 1584, when Dee and Kelly were in Cracow, Poland, that the bulk of the material typically associated with Enochian magick was transmitted. This included the Great Table of the Watchtowers, the Ninety-One Regions of the Earth, the Thirty Aethyrs, The Forty-Eight Calls (the last thirty of which are directly associated with the Thirty Aethyrs, and used in their scrying), The Vision of the Watchtowers, and the names of the Governors of the Thirty Aethyrs. Later still, in April 1587, Kelly received a revised version of the Great Table, in which some of the letters were changed and the position of the Elemental Tablets was moved.

Reading Dee's original diaries for the period covering these revelations is fascinating, and in some cases quite funny; you really get a sense of the drama and awe that both men felt as they received the angels' communications. From Dee's entry of Monday the 25th, 1584, describing the session that resulted in the receipt of the sigils (covering the Great Table) that spelled out the names of the Governors:

Kelly: 'Now come upon the square like Characters. They be the true Images of God his spiritual creatures.'
Dee: 'Write what thou feel.'
Kelly: 'I cannot.'
Dee: 'Endeavour to do your best, for he that biddeth you do will also give you power to do.'
Kelly: '. . . I perceive they be easy to make, for that I tell the squares by which the lines to pass, and draw from middle prick to middle prick . . . You heard one say, 'I write my own damnation.'
Dee: 'He might have said, you write *his* damnation. Pray and write as many more lines.'

Here Kelly seems to be struggling in his job as seer, first finding the receipt of the information difficult, and then worrying that he is being asked to 'write his own damnation'. Impatient to receive the angel's message, Dee urges his friend to persevere, and even suggests alternatives to the words Kelly heard in order to calm the man down. The 'pricks' Kelly refers to illustrate the way the sigils were received. Pricks of light appeared in the squares of the Great Table, which gradually darkened to form the symmetrical character being indicated. It sounds almost as if Kelly was witnessing an event similar to a Polaroid photograph being developed. Each sigil covered exactly seven squares, without ever overlapping a square occupied by another sigil. Thereafter Kelly was instructed to fill the grids with letters. It quickly became apparent to the men that if the course of the lines they had previously inserted were followed, the letters spelled out names – each beginning with a capital letter. There was a bigger surprise to follow, for shortly after they realised that they had just derived eighty-eight names, it became apparent that these were the names of most of the Governors of the ninety-one Parts of the Earth – names that they had already been given!

The Great Table (see Fig. 1) is of central importance to Enochian magick, containing as it does the names of the complete angelic hierarchy and the names of the Governors ruling the thirty Aethyrs (which thereby directly relates it to the Aethyrs themselves). The Aethyrs are conceived as different levels of spiritual experience, with the densest and most earthly at the 'bottom' and the most abstract and spiritual at the 'top'. They are as follows:

1.____Lil	11.____Ich	21.____Asp
2.____Arn	12.____Loe	22.____Lin
3.____Zom	13.____Zim	23.____Tor
4.____Paz	14.____Uta	24.____Nia
5.____Lit	15.____Oxo	25.____Uti
6.____Maz	16.____Lea	26.____Des
7.____Deo	17.____Tan	27.____Zaa
8.____Zid	18.____Zen	28.____Bag
9.____Zip	19.____Pop	29.____Rii
10.____Zax	20.____Chr	30.____Tex

ELEMENTAL TABLET   ELEMENTAL TABLET
OF AIR   OF EARTH

```
r Z i l a f A u t l p a e | b O a Z a R o p h a R a
a r d Z a i d p a L a m   | u N n a x o P S o n d n
c z o n s a r o Y a u b x | a i g r a n o o m a g g
T o i T x o t P a c o C a | o r p m n i n g b e a l
S i g a s o m r b z n h r | r s O n i z i r l e m u
f m o n d a T d i a r i p | i z i n r C z i a M h l
o r o i b A h a o z p i   | M O r d i a l h C t G a
c N a b r V i x q a z d h | R O c a n c h i a s o m
O i i i t T p a l O a i   | A r b i z m i i l p i z
A b a m o o o a C v c a c | O p a n a a L m S m a L
N a o c O T t n p r a T o | d O l o P i n i a n b a
o c a n m a g o t r o i m | r x p a o c s i z i x p
S h i a l r a p m z o x a | a x t i r V a s t r i m

m o t i b   a t n a n     | n a n t a   b i t o m

d o n p a T d a n V u a a | T a O A d u p t D n i m
o l o a G e o o b a v a   | a a b c o o r o m e b b
O P a m n o O G m d n m m | T o g c o n x m a l G m
a p l s T e d e c a o p o | n h o d D i a l e a o c
s c m i o o n A m l o x c | p a t A x i o V s P s W
V a r s G d L b r i a p h | S a a i x a a r V r o i
o i P t e a a p D o c e   | m p h a r s l g a i o l
p s u a n c r Z i r Z a p | M a m g l o i n L i r x
S i o d a o i n r z f m   | o l a a D a g a T a p a
d a l t T d n a d i r e r | p a L c o i d x P a c n
d i x o m o n s i o s p a | n d a z N x i V a a s a
O o D p z i A p a n l i x | i i d P o n s d A s p i
r g o a n n T A C r a r e x | r i n h t a r n d i ϑ
```

ELEMENTAL TABLET   ELEMENTAL TABLET
OF FIRE   OF WATER

Figure 1 The Great Table as Presented in 1584

The Great Table consists of four Watchtowers, each comprising a thirteen by twelve grid, and each Watchtower contains four sub-angles. The Golden Dawn attributed an element to each of the Watchtowers and sub-angles, and referred to the Watchtowers as 'Elemental Tablets'. As their terminology has been widely accepted by Enochian scholars I will use the terms Watchtowers and Elemental Tablets interchangeably throughout this book.

Three lines in each Tablet partition it into its four quarters, or sub-angles, and these are known as the line of the father, the line of the son and the line of the spirit. Symmetrically placed in each sub-angle is a 'calvary cross', which is six squares high and five wide. So, in summary, we have one Great Table, four Elemental Tablets and sixteen sub-angles. The squares that comprise the four Elemental Tablets are separated by the four names of the Tablet of Union – said to represent the highest spiritual forces – each repeated twice. These are: 'EXARP', 'HCOMA', BITOM' and NANTA'. The total number of squares in the Great Table is 624, increasing to 675 if you include the two lines on which the Holy Names of God appear.

The angels in due course gave the men instructions on how to derive from the Great Table a full angelic hierarchy. I won't provide a complete account of this derivation here – there are many excellent books out there that cover this ground – but to give readers a flavour of how it was done, I will show an extraction of the names of the Kings and six Seniors for the Elemental Tablet of Fire. Look again at Figure 1. The vertical line in the middle of the bottom left quadrant that begins 'teo' is the Line of the Father, the vertical line to the right of it is the line of the Son and the horizontal line beginning 'oip' the Line of the Holy Ghost. To derive the King's name, we start at the 'e' on the Line of the Holy Ghost which is immediately adjacent to the Line of the Father, and then move in a clockwise direction, up to the nearby 'd', and then along and around to end at the 'a' that was to the right of the starting 'e'. The resulting name is 'Edlprna'. For operations of severity the King's name would terminate with the letter to the left of the final 'a', but in this case this letter is also 'a', so the spelling is identical for both.

The six Seniors of each tablet are somewhat easier to locate. Their seven letter names extend out from the centre two letters of the Great Central Cross (the two lines that divide each Elemental Tablet into four quarters). In the case of the Elemental Tablet of Fire these are aaetPio (attributed to Mars), adoeoeT (Jupiter), aLndOod (Moon), arinnAP (Saturn), aapDoce (Venus) and Acodoin (Mercury).

As impressed as I and many others are with it, there are sceptics who have questioned the validity of Dee and Kelly's work. Perhaps their greatest charge – after 'magick isn't real' – is that in involving Kelly, Dee was working with a charlatan with 'form'. By the time Kelly met Dee, the former had already had his ears clipped for 'coining', or producing counterfeit money (an activity with close parallels to his desire to learn the art of turning lead into gold!), and he had left Oxford under a cloud.

Others have focused on the lack of results that Dee's work achieved. Although some of the predictions the angels made proved correct, others weren't. Alchemical secrets were sought but not divulged. Dee hoped to use his magickal workings to discover the secrets of the legendary Book of Soyga, but these were not revealed.

A further strand of attack focuses on the angelic language imparted to the pair. Although some linguists are impressed by its apparent syntax and grammar, others are of the opinion that it is a fabricated tongue. On the subject of language, some commentators have also pointed out the 'convenience' of the use of Latin (which Kelly understood) as opposed to Greek and Hebrew (which he didn't) by the angels as proof that the information was coming from the younger man as opposed to a supernatural source.

If forced to lay my cards on the table, I'll admit that I have two working hypotheses for what the angelic revelations of Dee and Kelly represent, which I alternate between (and will discuss later on), but let's deal firstly with the points raised above. Regarding Kelly's honesty, I have already stated that the man's gifts as a seer may have predisposed him to being economical with the truth and something of a fantasist. I'm in effect turning this argument on its head, and saying that the fact that he was a bit of a rogue makes the validity of the messages he received *more* believable, not less so. In terms of the results of Dee's workings, something that has to be borne in mind is that Dee's agenda may well have been at odds with that of the angels. It may be that far from being interested in helping him crack the mystery of the Book of Soyga, they wished to impart something far more important – a means of spiritual development. The very fact that this book is being written can be seen as proof that in this respect they succeeded. And as for the genuineness of 'Enochian' as a language, it would appear that neither those that accept this nor those that don't have been able to prove their view conclusively, so this debate perhaps has to be set aside until such time as stronger arguments for or against are made.

CHAPTER NINE

My interest in Enochian magick started about ten years after my willed exploration of spiritual matters began, and I was inspired to follow in Dee's footsteps by an appreciation the shamanic tradition. I have always felt that magick has to be experienced, not just read about, and the shamanic way, which focuses largely on vision-questing and getting 'stuck in' has always struck me as being much more powerful and transformative than say, studying Hebrew Qabalistic gematria. Shamanism was appealing, but I have always believed that we in the West should explore our own shamanic tradition. There seems to me to be something slightly bogus about white Caucasians 'connecting' with the African or South American spiritual traditions – traditions that surely resonate most strongly amongst people indigenous to those parts of the world. We in the West have to have our own shamanic way; the question being, what *is* that tradition?

It may be tempting to propose druidism or Wicca as representing the nearest thing Westerners have to a native shamanic path, but I'm not so sure. They are undoubtedly spiritual approaches that 'belong' to the British Isles and parts of the Continent, but they represent forms of spiritual practice that are so ancient that I'm not sure whether they can be said to have much relevance to modern Britons or Westerners generally. Few of us, living in our double-glazed, centrally-heated homes, have much understanding or appreciation of the elements or nature. We might think we do, through watching the odd wildlife documentary, or the once-a-decade camping trip, but for the most part Spring Festivals and solar adorations have as little relevance to us as totem worship.

So where should we Westerners look for *our* shamanic heritage? Well, I'd say that the ceremonial magick tradition of Western Europe, and especially as inspired by John Dee, represents as close to a true vision-questing tradition as we have. John Dee was at the cutting edge of the technology of his day – he was a mathematician, a pioneer of navigational methods, and a man who was at home with tables, grids and ciphers. In this respect he would have been quite comfortable in our modern society, with its emphasis on information and its diagrammatic representation. John Dee's magickal legacy is one of spiritual questing that can be mapped and charted, via concepts such as the thirty Aethyrs and the Elemental Tablets. It is true that the Qabalah provides us with the Tree of Life, which is a diagrammatic representation of the universe analogous to the concentric circles of the Aethyrs, but in the Great Table Enochian magick provides a far greater degree of sophistication through its modularity. The Great Table can be meditated on in its entirety, but also broken down into increasingly smaller elements – the Elemental Tablets, the sub-angles of the Elemental Tablets, and through to the angelic hierarchy. We can continue right down to the individual letters of the table in our search for the very building blocks of the magickal universe.

Ceremonial magick has been the source of much confusion over the years, stemming from a misunderstanding of the processes involved. When I first tried to evoke a spirit, I expected to see the entity appear in the triangle that had been placed outside my circle, and be so unequivocally present I could smell its bad breath. In a powerful ritual there may be some energetic disturbances in the temple, but spirits never appear in any sort of physical form before the magician. How can they? They don't have a physical body. What the magician *may* see is an astral impression of the entity – if he has some clairvoyant ability – and thus we see straightaway the link between ceremonial magick and the shamanic experience. In evoking or invoking a spirit, the magician is simply conducting a highly formalised visionquest. The fact that the magus may have a request to ask of the spirit in no way distinguishes it from shamanism, as very often the shaman undertakes his spirit journeying in order to heal someone, or gain information.

And so it was through trying to find a shamanic tradition that suited my background, psychology and cultural heritage that I came to appreciate the value of the Enochian system. My first explorations involved a sequential scrying of the Thirty Aethyrs, beginning at the innermost, Tex, and working up to Lil. As previously mentioned, the Aethyrs are represented diagrammatically as thirty concentric rings, with the Aethyrs becoming increasingly more abstract and spiritual as we move outward. It is customarily stated that it is 'easier' to scry the lower Aethyrs, and that as we progress upwards they become harder to penetrate. I suspect that this is a notion that was first espoused by An Important Occultist, and has since been proved to be true largely because expectation has guided practitioners' experiences. For my part, I have not found this to be the case, and in fact my scrying sessions became more vivid and detailed as I progressed upwards.

Before going on to give a description of a typical scrying session, I think it would be useful to discuss exactly what scrying is. Conceptions of what the practice consists of range from losing yourself in a daydream to a state in which one is so totally immersed in the astral world that all awareness of the physical plane disappears. Kelly scryed using a crystal or an obsidian stone, but others use bowls of ink, glasses of water, or simply the blackness one sees when one closes one's eyes. How you do it is, quite frankly, irrelevant – these media are just tools to allow the Magician to tap into that 'something' that is the basis of shamanic journeying. Everything, from light daydreaming to full astral immersion, can be considered scrying, though obviously the more altered one is – the deeper the dialogue with the subconscious and via its agency the astral realm – the greater the quality of information you are likely to receive. This is where the importance of meditational and hypnotic techniques comes in – unless you a naturally highly psychic, you need to spend some time 'altering' yourself prior to attempting to scry, in order to ensure you get worthwhile results. One way of entering an altered state of consciousness is through drugs – and I will explore this possibility later – though this method is not without its dangers.

When people first attempt to scry, especially if they have not entered a sufficiently strong trance state beforehand, they will often find that the mental images they get lack sufficient reality tone, and they may find they are doing little more than letting their mind wander, with the knowledge of what they are 'meant' to be seeing meaning that they do in fact see the occasional scarab, golden lion or truncated pyramid. This is not satisfactory, and the magician is advised to spend more time practicing his visualisation skills, along with learning how to enter trance states. If you are reasonably altered, however, there is nothing wrong with giving your vision a little 'push'. If all you see at first is blackness, imagine yourself to be walking along a long narrow tunnel. Visualise a door at the end of it, and yourself opening it. You still might not 'see' anything. What you need to do in such instances is imagine what you *might* see. A mental picture arises, and if you are sufficiently altered a string of further images should be triggered. If everything goes to plan, before long a point will arise where images are arising spontaneously. You are now starting to properly scry. Go deeper still and characters you encounter will start to interact with you with autonomy. They appear very much as 'other' to yourself and can incite fear, love and curiosity, just as another person you might meet in normal life can.

The CIA's remote viewing experiments, which ran for many years, were basically a scrying programme. Interestingly, in its early days, much emphasis was placed on elaborate ways of 'targeting' the visions operatives were to receive. Co-ordinates were used, as if each human is equipped with some sort of mental GPS system which enables them to 'lock on' to a particular point on the earth. Our subconscious mind is far cleverer than that, however. It's enough to say to a skilled scryer, 'I want you to focus on whatever it is I'm thinking about', without indicating whether it is a person, place or concept that is being thought of. When applying this principle to scrying the Aethyrs, we can see that just knowing which Aethyr it is you wish to explore is sufficient to 'get you there'. The ritual steps and paraphernalia that are used are important to help induce a state of trance, but are not part of any means of 'unlocking' the door to a given Aethyr. There's no password, no buttons to press, just a desire to go there, coupled with a state of gnosis.

One of the great proofs of the existence of the thirty Aethyrs is that many people have travelled to them, and there is broad agreement on the experiences each provide. I am well aware of the power of suggestion and anticipation in matters of astral exploration, and so before I began my investigation of the Aethyrs I deliberately avoided reading about them. I knew that Tex was the densest, most material Aethyr, and Lil the most abstract and spiritual region, but beyond that, nothing. I was keen to avoid the 'contamination' reading others' accounts of the Aethyrs would create because I wanted to be able to assess the validity of the Enochian spiritual model. Self-delusion and wishful thinking plague many occult experiences, and I wanted to be as free from these as possible.

So, with much anticipation, and a little trepidation, I found myself one afternoon setting up my temple in anticipation of a journey to Tex. I had photocopies of the four Elemental Tablets, a lamen and Ring of Solomon (both made by laminating photocopies of the original design), and had my Sigillum dei Aemeth and planetary sigils to hand. I opened with a lesser banishing ritual, and followed this with a recitation of the Forty-Eighth call (in both English and Enochian). Then, after vibrating the names of the four Governors ruling Tex, I induced gnosis through pranayama and 'not thinking'. I should mention that a 'normal' exploration of an Aethyr would involve the Magician moving straight to scrying after the vibration of the Governors' names. This, I believe, is a mistake, unless the magician is already mentally altered through drugs, fasting or brain chemistry – schizophrenics probably don't need to bother with meditation prior to scrying! As mentioned above, when attempting to converse with spirits or penetrate spiritual realms, it is imperative that the practitioner is in a state of consciousness that allows easy communication with the subconscious. The symbols that our subconscious resonates to can be viewed as a metaphysical programming language, and unless you are in a state in which you can use this language, progress in astral or spiritual practices will be poor.

It took me probably fifteen minutes to reach a state that I considered suitable for the task at hand. At this point I again mentally repeated the Governors' names, then visualised a door with the name 'Tex' on it. Now in my imaginary or light body, I opened the door, and stepped into 'Texas'. I immediately found myself in a rural landscape, standing by the tall stone walls of a medieval castle. I was on a path that led downhill, away from the fortress which was to my right. I should mention that this sort of starting point is typical for me when exploring the Aethyrs. I normally find myself in a setting where nature is on display – often in the form of a wood, a beach or a meadow. I've never entered an Aethyr and found myself in a supermarket, for example. That isn't to say that a session that involved a modern setting wouldn't be valid, of course. The Aethyrs are not age-specific.

In this first scrying session I had some trouble manipulating my imaginary body and focusing my vision. I guess it was something like the sensation that would be experienced if a small boy suddenly found himself in the body of a large man; I could move my limbs, but in a clunky fashion. There was also a lag time between wanting to look in a particular direction and actually doing so, as if my astral eyes weren't quite as fast as my astral mind.

On finding myself in this landscape, the first thought that occurred to me was, 'Now what?' Exploration was the name of the game, and the castle seemed the logical place to start. I turned around and walked up the path to the castle gates. These huge doors would not yield for me, but there was a smaller door to the right of these that was, conveniently, open. I entered through this. The four walls of the castle overlooked a large and spacious courtyard; the rooms of the castle were contained within the walls themselves. As I walked across the courtyard I found myself suddenly engulfed in a thick mist. It was so dense that I couldn't see more than a couple of feet in either direction. I looked down, and noticed my feet for the first time. They were shod in heavy, crudely-made boots. I'm not an expert on the history of footwear, but they looked like they were made in a medieval style – certainly by 1700 I imagine the basic standard of footwear would have been much higher.

You'll notice that I still hadn't been accosted at this stage by flaming golden griffins or three headed Babalon-whores. At the risk of incurring the wrath of the entire Thelemite community, I have sometimes wondered whether Crowley's accounts of scrying the Aethyrs as documented in 'The Vision and the Voice' did not benefit from a little editing and amplification. Call me a cynic, but the way I see it, the Aethyrs don't really care about the scryer's agenda; the experience they provide exists outside the practitioner's hopes and desires, and although there is always some 'colouring' provided by an individual's subconscious, when this starts to intrude too forcibly onto the visionary experience you have to question the validity of the vision. It seems to me that in 'The Vision and the Voice' Crowley was to some extent trying to provide further corroboration of his Aiwass experience.

Anyway, back to my first experience of Tex. After finding myself surrounded by thick mist, I decided that my best bet was to walk forwards with my arms outstretched, in the knowledge that sooner or later I would hit one of the castle's four walls. After finding a section of wall I could then feel my way to one of the doors I had earlier seen that the walls contained. You might wonder why I wanted to protect myself from stumbling into anything, given that all of this was happening in my 'mind'. The answer is that whilst scrying, it is very easy to forget that the experience isn't really happening, and I didn't want to experience even the pain that might come from bumping my astral head.

In due course my hands felt cold stone, and I then began to walk in line with the wall, soon coming to a large arched doorway. I entered through this, and found myself at the foot of a spiralling staircase, which I began to ascend. I could see quite clearly by this stage, but couldn't identify the source of light. I saw neither windows nor lamps. I arrived at a first floor, but for some reason felt compelled to carry on up the stairs. When I got to the second floor I left the staircase, and began wandering down a long corridor. The floors were wooden, the walls stone, and there seemed nothing in the way of decoration. I might have been exploring a medieval dungeon. I became aware that I was passing doors on my left, and it was apparent that I could choose to enter whichever of them I wanted to. I carried on for a few moments, then at random chose to open a particular door. Inside was a table and chair. On the table was a single lit candle, along with a plate of food. It looked as if someone had been eating a meal in the room until just a few moments before. For some reason at this point I began to feel fear, even though there was no obvious reason for this emotion. Looking up, I got a shock when I saw that what looked like an owl was partially protruding from the wall. It was as if the owl had grown out of the stone of the wall – its flesh was intermingled with, and part of, the rock. I knew that the protocol was that I should address the owl – it could well be one of the Governors of the Aethyr – but my sense of fear increased yet further, and I brought myself out of my trance.

So ended my first exploration of Tex. I was annoyed with myself for aborting the session prematurely, but pleased that this had only happened because of the intensity of the experience. I had proved to myself that the realm I had penetrated had an objective existence – as far as anything that is accessed via consciousness alone can have, anyway. There was certainly no question of me having 'forced' my vision – it arose with total spontaneity. I was tempted to straightaway compare what I had seen with the accounts of others who had visited Tex, but decided to hold off until I had experienced a full scrying session of one of the Aethyrs.

My experience of the Aethyrs became more vivid over time, confirming that scrying is an art that benefits from practice. I had particularly powerful results when scrying the 23rd Aethyr, Tor. I gained access to the Aethyr through a door that bore the number '23'. Immediately on passing through this door I found myself in total blackness, and aware that I was falling through space. This falling sensation carried on for so long that I had begun to wonder whether this was all I would experience, when I suddenly hit the ground. I found I was on a snow-covered mountain slope. It was late afternoon, and the light was fading. I found a path, and followed this downhill, eventually being led to a cave with a low ceiling. Crouched at the entrance to the cave was an animal that looked like a cross between a monkey and a cat. It had the size and body of a monkey, but its eyes and nose were definitely feline, and it lacked the pronounced brow of an ape. Bizarrely, the creature was clothed in a tan coloured robe.

The 'conkey' looked quite threatening, but when it became aware of my presence it itself became alarmed, scurrying around erratically as if it had the energy to escape, but no idea of which direction to take in fleeing. Eventually the beast calmed down, returning to a sitting position, and looking at me directly. I sensed it was trying to communicate with me. I struggled to open up some sort of telepathic contact with the animal, but all I got was the strong sense that I should follow it. No sooner had this impression been received, than it turned around and began to walk into the cave. I duly followed. The conkey led me through the stone tunnel, which narrowed quickly to become just wide enough for me to squeeze through. After what seemed like fifteen minutes of walking I saw daylight, and soon found myself standing on the edge of a steep precipice, craggy rocks visible below.

The scene changed abruptly, and now I was walking along a path that followed the course of huge city walls. To my left was a gorge through which a river ran, and up ahead was a bridge, which spanned the gorge and terminated at gates that gave entry to the fortified city. I realised for the first time that the monkey cat had disappeared, and that I was on my own. I got onto the road leading up to the city gates, and found myself one of many pedestrians walking into the settlement. Looking around, I saw that everyone seemed to be dressed in a Middle Eastern style – all long robes and headscarves. Many of my fellow pedestrians were wearing one-piece black outfits that covered everything – heads and faces included, with just a small slit to see through, and which reminded me of women in a niqab. I found the people so attired quite threatening.

Through the gates I went and down a long thoroughfare which had shops and stalls on either side. It was very busy, as if I had arrived on market day. For some reason I decided to duck into one of the shops lining this main road, finding myself in a linen store. Rolls of fabric were piled high on shelves, and samples of the wares being sold were spread out on a couple of tables. The shop didn't have a conventional door; instead, a cloth curtain gave access to it.

After a few moments I noticed that there was a woman sitting in the shop – the owner presumably. She stood, and I was immediately entranced by her beauty. She reminded me of a Hollywood screen siren – something about her colouring and hairstyle I think. There were shadows on her face that didn't seem to correspond with the way the light fell, almost as if her face was tattooed – though this was definitely not the case. The woman had an archetypal quality about her – though I couldn't decide which archetype this might be – queen, perhaps, or enchantress. I was in awe of her beauty.

I asked her if I could sit in her shop for a while, and she agreed to this. Grabbing a stool by the door, I watched the feet of those that walked past the shop – these being visible because the curtain over the store's doorway hung about six inches off the ground. I say feet – in most cases it *was* feet I was looking at – but I also saw the hooves of cattle and sheep, and in one case some outlandishly large paws that must have belonged to a huge beast.

After a while My Lady – this is how I felt I should refer to her – came over to where I sat and placed a cloak over my shoulder. I wasn't cold, so I was confused as to why she should feel compelled to do this. Not for long though, as she placed a hand on my shoulder, indicating to me with this simple gesture that I should leave. The sense wasn't that I was being ejected; more that it was time for me to see other things.

I left the shop and joined the crowd walking down the street outside. I quickly noticed that everyone was walking in the same direction – away from the city gates. The main thoroughfare we were on sloped upwards, and as I looked ahead I could see the crest of a hill. I realised that I and my fellow pedestrians were all heading for this distant summit. I sensed great purpose in those that walked, as if we were all nearing the end of a long and perilous pilgrimage.

As we continued up the hill the shops and houses fell away, and we walked through a barren, rocky landscape. It started to become much hotter, and it suddenly dawned on me that we were walking up a volcano, heading for its still-active top. As I got nearer still, I could see that those ahead of me were not stopping when they reached the summit – they seemed to be toppling straight into the heart of the volcano. At this point I realised I would have to choose whether to follow them, and the decision seemed to be much more important than one of life or death; it seemed I would be making a spiritual commitment of some sort if I chose to fling myself into the lava. In due course I reached the lip of the volcano crater, and without hesitation flung myself into it. There was a blinding flash when I hit the molten rock, but no pain, and then I found myself falling, falling . . . until suddenly I discovered that I was swimming through crystal clear and beautifully cold water. I swam upwards, breaking the surface to find myself swimming about a hundred metres from a small tropical island. Here the vision ended.

By the time I experienced this Aethyr I was diligently comparing my findings with those of other explorers (though never reading others' accounts before my scrying of a given Aethyr), and finding there were often startling similarities. The Internet is of course a great place to track down both conventionally and electronically published accounts of scrying, and in looking for others' experience of Tor I quickly came across one person's

record that had been posted on the website 'thebaptistshead.
co.uk'. From the fifth paragraph: 'I am inside a volcano, in a
lake of molten rock. The molten rock is my body. There is a
nun dressed in white, coming toward me in the fire. Her cloak
billows madly. She carries a lantern and a staff.' Further on:
'Now I see a beautiful woman, dressed in a kimono. She takes
off her clothes and reveals her radiant wings.'

I sat bolt upright when I read about the volcano in this
account: not typical occult imagery, and not only does the scryer
encounter a volcano, but like myself, he enters it. In looking
for evidence of semi-permanent scenery for Tor, this seemed
highly promising. I and another scryer had shared a very similar
specific experience. I was also interested to note the presence
of a beautiful woman in this account, though had to concede
that humans were likely to be a very common feature in scrying
sessions.

Further trawling uncovered the following account of the same
Aethyr, from a Frater DD, who has published a number of his
Enochian ritual records at 'mysteryofbabylon.com':

'TOR, TOR, TOR . . .
I am looking up, from within a crater, the sky is yellow, as I
look down, there is darkness within the crater, the ground is
lit from the sunlight above.
There is a bubbling pool, possibly of lava, flowing out of it in
a small stream . . .'

Here we find more volcanic imagery, and further confirmation
that all three of us were treading the same path in our exploration of the 23rd Aethyr. I was curious to know what images
of lava and volcanoes might signify in the context of an astral
journey to this region, and therefore moved from spotting these
similarities of experience to looking at what each of the Aethyrs
are meant to represent in spiritual terms. In doing so I had to
bear in mind that much has been written about the meaning of
the Aethyrs by different authors, but that the angels themselves
were silent on this matter – at no time did they impart to Dee

and Kelly a crib list of significances for each of the Aethyrs. Caution was necessary to avoid blindly accepting what would be nothing more than opinion on this matter.

One description of the experience of Tor is 'Stability in Change', and certainly the volcano seems an apt symbol for this. A volcano is a fixed geographical feature which mediates the upwelling of lava from the earth's crust – the volcano is a stable feature, which enables change in the form of fluctuating lava outflows. Volcanoes can also create stability in the form of new islands through the outpouring of lava.

Many occultists have tried to map the Aethyrs to the Tree of Life; understandable given the popularity of the Qabalistic model as a means of mapping not just spiritual, but also mental, emotional and physical experience. How, though, to fit the thirty Aethyrs onto the Tree of Life, with its ten Sephiroth and thirty-two paths? If only there were thirty paths, or thirty Sephiroth! Some have allocated each three consecutive Aethrys to each of the Sephiroth. This, to my mind, seems wrong. Three sequential Aethyrs will involve different, often contradictory, impulses and lessons. Aleister Crowley's method centred around the ninety-one Governors of the Aethyrs. He envisaged the four Governors of Tex occupying the four lowest Sephiroth, with the three Governors of RII occupying Tiphareth, Geburah and Chesed and the Governors of BAG occupying the three highest Sephiroth. When it came to mapping the remaining Aethyrs, he saw all twenty-seven remaining Aethyrs being located in Malkuth on a second, higher, Tree of Life, with the Governors of the three highest Aethyrs (LIL, ARN and ZOM) occupying the remaining Sephiroth.

I find this approach somewhat contrived. My personal view coincides with that of the Golden Dawn: if we take the Aethyrs as primarily representing non-material experience, the easiest mapping method is to assign them by moving up the Tree of Life, so that Tex is located in Malkuth, RII in Yesod, and BAG in Hod, etc., with this first batch of ten Aethyrs being mapped to an Astral Tree of Life. CHR through ICH would then be matched with Sephiroth from Malkuth to Kether, and to a

Mental Tree of Life, and ZAX to LIL likewise, to a Spiritual Tree of Life.

If this method is correct, TOR would map to Binah on an Astral Tree of Life. So how does this shed light on my and others' experience of this Aethyr? Well, straight off you will recall that one of the most significant aspects of my scrying session was an encounter with a woman – a woman who cloaked me and gave me temporary shelter after my arrival in the city. Also, after plunging into the volcano, I eventually emerged into the sea. The sea and a mothering woman – the two most common symbols of Binah!

Let's see if this Tree of Life correspondence method works with another of my scrying experiences. On my first exploration of TAN, the seventeenth Aethyr, the vision began with me standing in a landscape of newly harvested fields. To my right was a tree with very dark green leaves. These I found so intriguing and desirable I couldn't help myself grabbing a handful of them, which I then crushed and smeared all over my face. They had a sharp but somehow pleasant smell. After this strange action, I happened to look down, and noticed that the soil was hot and dry.

Moments later I had a strong urge to hide, without knowing what or whom I might be concealing myself from. I ducked behind a nearby bale of hay. Soon a man on horseback came into view, and as he neared me I could see he was dressed all in black. The horse, also, was black. The horsemen stopped by the bale of hay, and it was immediately apparent that he knew I was there. I stood up and looked at him. He was white, but his face was smeared with black and red paint, in what looked like ceremonial or battle adornment. I sensed that this was Aydropt, one of the Aethyr's Governors.

'I am but a shadow of my true self,' Aydropt informed me.

I acknowledged this statement with a nod, then said, 'Can I ride with you?'

He agreed, and I mounted behind him. We set off, and soon were galloping at speed across the land. After some time Aydropt halted his horse, and looking ahead I could see that we had arrived at the edge of a vast cliff. A wild, blue sea crashed against rocks a great distance below us, and extended before us as far as the eye could see.

'Do we turn back, or carry on?' Aydropt asked.

'Carry on,' I said, wondering what had possessed me to answer in this way.

The horse jumped off the cliff. I was convinced we were doomed, but no sooner had the horse leapt than it sprouted wings. These flapped powerfully, and we flew easily.

Suddenly it became dark, and ahead I could see a tall castle that occupied the whole of a small island. Aydropt had changed form now. His head was green and vaguely reptilian. I shouted my discovery to him, and he replied: 'Maybe I have changed, or maybe your eyes have changed.'

Soon we landed in the central courtyard of the castle, and were quickly surrounded by many small creatures. They looked like nothing I had seen before – something like a cross between an owl and a small furry mammal. I dismounted, and the small creatures led me across the courtyard to the entrance to a large dining hall. I was shown to my seat in the dining room, which was full of other similar creatures, all busy feasting. As I waited for my food to arrive I asked the creature to the right of me who they were as a species. He didn't answer my question, saying, 'We know of you humans, but you do not much interest us.'

This response seemed to dent my appetite, because I asked to be shown the room I somehow knew had been allocated to me. One of the creatures stood up and led me out of the dining hall, along a corridor, up some stairs, and finally to my chamber. The room had a stone floor and walls.

No sooner had I been left alone in the room than my awareness of it faded, and I saw a succession of seemingly unrelated images. First I saw a cold, rocky mountain top; it was raining heavily. Then an image of a gutted rabbit appeared. It was being hung upside down by its feet. I saw a meteor, moving swiftly though space. Finally, I saw a seedling, pushing upwards from the soil.

Using the system outlined above, the Seventeenth Aethyr

relates to Netzach, and Netzach as it manifests on the Mental Plane. Straightaway we can see that my vision accords with such a view, abounding as it does with images of fertility and nature. The colour green is emphasised, as are the processes of growth (the image of the seedling) and harvest. I saw Netzach manifested in its more mental or abstract form by witnessing the cycle of growth and death (via the vision of the dead rabbit, and of a seedling germinating).

How have others experienced this Aethyr? A Duncan from baptistshead.co.uk, describing a pyramid he finds himself in, writes: 'There's a spirit here that we've found before: an angle. It tells me that there are hidden enclaves that we haven't encountered yet. They have some important teachings that we haven't encountered. Where do we find them? The answer comes back: the symbol of an owl.'

Recall that my experience of this Aethyr involves meeting with creatures that resemble a cross between an owl and a furry animal. Do owls correspond to this Aethyr? Well, interestingly, 'The Little Owl' of Greek mythology was associated with the Goddess Athena, who herself is attributed to Netzach.

The account of scrying the Aethyrs that is given the most attention is of course Crowley's 'The Vision and The Voice', a record of the visions he received whilst travelling in the Algerian desert in 1909. I have found this book a great resource when looking for shared symbolism in my Enochian workings, and it is undoubtedly a work of poetic beauty. I would, however, re-emphasise my earlier point about exercising a degree of caution when assessing this work. If one's scrying visions do not measure up to those of Crowley's in terms of dramatic quality and symbolic content, that does not mean that you have failed to penetrate a given Aethyr. Crowley's visions were received through his 'filter', and it is an undeniable fact that we can appreciate the man's huge contribution to magick and also understand that he suffered from a degree of ego inflation which made everything he perceived take on a sense of huge importance and destiny. I imagine that he couldn't take a shower without hearing an angelic chorus, and that opening a jar of marmalade could easily have had mystical overtones for him. For this reason, I think a contemporary Magician is probably better off comparing his experiences with the Aethyrs to those of other contemporary Magicians.

In line with my view that the exploration of the Aethyrs represents a form of Western Shamanism, I believe that in the right context the use of mind-altering substances can be beneficially used to heighten the visionary experience for the Magician. Cannabis will aid entry to the astral, but the drug that I think stands out as being the best to use for scrying sessions is salvia divinorum. Salvia in higher doses is capable of effects that make LSD seem mild – total depersonalisation, the sense of melding with inanimate objects, the experience of vistas that words can't even describe – and it has the distinct benefit of having effects that only last a relatively short period of time. Salvia is certainly capable of taking the Magician to a place where his scrying sessions will take on a degree of reality that is comparable to waking reality – a good analogy would be that instead of an experience akin to watching a film, the magician 'steps into the film'.

I used salvia as part of my scrying of the 25th Aethyr, VTI, and also the 24th Aethyr, NIA. The experience involving the 25th Aethyr was absolutely remarkable. Having done my banishings, and recited my calls and Governors' names, I took three or four puffs of a x5 concentration salvia preparation. Most salvia that is consumed in the West is in a concentrated form, but as concentrations go up to x50, the concoction I was smoking was relatively mild. Nevertheless, within about twenty seconds of my last lungful of smoke, I lost all awareness of my physical surroundings, and found myself in what looked to be a totally unfamiliar room, in the presence of a woman who could only be described as an 'hag'. She was thoroughly repulsive to look at, with a large warty nose, protruding, hairy chin, lined face, and thinning, grey hair. I would have expected to find the sight of this woman terrifying, but instead I accepted her presence quite happily and sensed just curiosity on her part. Although I'd temporarily lost all touch with my physical temple, I hadn't forgotten my purpose in taking salvia, nor that I was in the middle of a scrying session. I became aware that my ritual had attracted this woman – whoever she was – and using telepathy I asked her what she wanted. The response I got was that she 'was just passing through' and was simply interested to see what I was up to. The woman did attempt to communicate something to me about the nature of the working I was doing, but to my everlasting annoyance I don't remember what this was. In hindsight I wish I had asked her many of the interesting questions I can now think of putting to her, but I didn't, and our encounter consisted largely of staring placidly at each other, before the effects of the drug faded and I returned to a more-or-less normal state of consciousness. After the strongest effects of the salvia had worn off I attempted to continue with conventional scrying, but I have to admit to finding it difficult to relax and focus sufficiently. I was just too excited by my encounter with the hag.

In the days following this experience I tried to determine whether visions of an old crone have any particular significance to the 25th Aethyr, but couldn't find any suggestion of this in the books I consulted. Interestingly, a week later I scryed the 24th Aethyr, taking exactly the same dose of salvia as I had with the 25th, but this time, although I was as strongly affected by the drug, I didn't have any visions of crones or anyone else. I can't say with any certainty who the old lady might have been. Perhaps she was one of the Governors of the 25th Aethyr, and I just didn't recognise her as such. It might be that she was an earthbound spirit who happened to be wandering the neighbourhood as I was scrying, and the salvia opened me up enough to perceive her. Whilst her identity I will never know for sure, the experience I had of meeting her is one I will never forget!

CHAPTER TEN

My experiences of scrying the Aethyrs focused the interest I already had in Enochian magick until it would be fair to say that I pretty much became obsessed. In particular I developed a fascination for the Great Table, which seemed to hint at mysteries beyond those that had been revealed to Dee and Kelly.

It was at around this time that the memory of the lucid dream I had had at the age of 24 came back – the one in which I had seen what looked like a periodic table under circumstances that were similar to the original Enochian revelations – and the thought occurred to me that the Great Table might be a sort of 'spiritual periodic table'. Many of the letters that occupy the squares of the Table are themselves used to denote chemical elements – what, I wondered, if the squares were keys to divine wisdom in a manner akin to representing the building blocks of spiritual existence? The near-universal acceptance of the assignation of a different element to each of the Watchtowers, and to the sub-angles of the Watchtowers, seemed to hint at this. The Golden Dawn even developed a system whereby each individual square is assigned its own elemental composition. I was reminded of the book find years before, when I had gone to the home of a recent suicide. That man's diary had been my first introduction to the term 'Enochian', and I remembered the entry that had mentioned the chemical processes behind the decomposition of leaves. It seemed I was being given some pretty big clues.

How to explore this hunch? I couldn't use the scientific method, but nor did meditating on a letter from the Great Table in the hope it might give up its secrets seem appropriate either. I began to research the periodic table, learning that it has expanded over time from Plato's 'Earth, Fire, Water, Air' through to the 118 elements that currently comprise it. The list has expanded largely through the discovery of new elements, but also with the creation of some synthetic elements. Debate continues as to how many naturally occurring elements there are, with some being more selective than others in classifying an element as such. Some elements have only been observed in laboratory conditions; others such as elements 85 and 87 appear in nature but only fleetingly. Anywhere between 88 and 94 elements are accepted as naturally occurring, depending on the definition you use. The average of 88 and 94 is, intriguingly, 91 – the number of Governors of the Thirty Aethyrs! Now, the Governors rule the 91 parts of the Earth – but isn't 'parts of the Earth' one way of describing the elements? Interestingly, some believe there to be a 92nd Governor, Paraoan, whose name is spelt using the letters in the Great Table that remain unused after the 91 'regular' Governors' names have been spelt out, and chemistry primers will tend to give 92 as the number of naturally occurring elements. (As a curious aside, the name of the 93rd element is Neptunium – quite apt given Crowley's fondness for mysticism, magick and morphine and the fact that this element was discovered in 1940, during his lifetime.)

If even more confirmation were needed that The Great Table should be considered to behave like a spiritual periodic table, consider the words of the Angel Ave, as given in Casaubon's 'A True & Faithful Relation . . .':

Ave: Now to the purpose: Rest, for the place is holy. First, generally what this table containeth.

1. All human knowledge.
2. Out of it springeth Physick.
3. The knowledge of all elemental Creatures amongst you. How many kinds there are, and for what they were created. Those that live in the air, by themselves. Those that live in the waters, by themselves. Those that dwell in

the earth, by themselves. The property of the fire – which is the secret of all things.
4. The knowledge, finding and use of metals.
   The virtue of them.
   The congelations and virtues of stones.
5. The conjoining and knitting together of Natures. The destruction of Nature, and of things that may perish.
6. Moving from place to place.
7. The knowledge of all crafts Mechanical.
8. Transmutatio formalis, fed non effentialis.

Of particular interest are points 4 and 8. Point 4 refers to the 'finding and use of metals' and the 'congelations and virtues of stones'. 'Congelation' is the process of knitting together, as good a description as I can think of for the processes behind the chemical composition of matter. Point 8 refers to the alchemical process of transmuting one substance into another. It is interesting to note that whilst neither scientists nor alchemists have been able to transmute literal lead into literal gold, some of the 118 elements in the periodic table are synthetic – there has been transmutation of one element into another.

The elements of the physical periodic table are arranged by atomic number, with this number relating to the number of electrons orbiting the nucleus of the atom. The higher the atomic number the greater the weight of the atom, so of the naturally occurring elements Uranium (92) is the heaviest, and Hydrogen (1) the lightest. Could it be that there is a direct mapping of Governors to elements? In this manner LIL's three Governors and Parts of Earth governed should relate to the lightest and least 'earthy' elements, and we would match Occodon with Hydrogen (1), Pascomb with Helium (2), and Valgars with Lithium (3). Hydrogen, as a rocket fuel, helium as a balloon gas and lithium, the lightest of all metals, would seem to sit comfortably with LIL.

Iron we would expect to have fiery associations, due to its attribution to Mars. Looking at the periodic table we can see that it has the atomic number 26. The twenty-sixth Governor is

Cralpir, of ZIP, and ZIP is associated with the element of fire via its placement in the Elemental Tablet of Fire.

Just when it would seem that there can't possibly be more confirmation that we're on to something here, let's return to the layout of the Elemental Tablets, which are twelve squares across and thirteen squares down. The Great Table is in some senses a mandala, and it had always struck me as odd that it is not perfectly symmetrical. Thinking about this led to me reaching for my calculator, and you can imagine my surprise when I discovered that dividing twelve by thirteen we get the decimal 0.92. 92 is of course the number of naturally occurring elements by some definitions, and exactly the number of Governors if we include Paraoan!

Returning briefly to Plato, with his division of matter into four elements, each corresponding to one of the five Platonic solids, he also anticipated the element 'spirit' – or 'ether' by having a platonic solid 'left over' after allocating one each to 'earth', 'water', 'fire' and 'air'. To get technical for a second, a Platonic solid is a convex polyhedron that is regular (in the sense of a regular polygon). The faces of a Platonic solid are congruent regular solids, with the same number of faces meeting at each vertex. The Platonic solid that would be allocated to 'ether' is the icosahedron, which intriguingly, has thirty faces – one for each of the Aethyrs!

If we accept that the Great Table is a type of spiritual periodic table, the question that arises is, 'How do we use it?' I believe that this is where the scrying of each of the thirty Aethyrs can be seen to be of supreme importance – in effecting an alchemical transformation of the individual. Remember that each Aethyr is governed by three or four Governors, with the sigils of the Governors (created by connecting the squares that spell their name with a line) covering almost all the squares in the Great Table. By scrying each of the Aethyrs, working from Tex upwards, the Magician can be said to be absorbing the energies of the entire Table, with a resultant transformation of his or her psyche or spiritual nature. He or she turns spiritual lead into spiritual gold.

Trying to identify 'spiritual elements' in the manner that scientists have isolated physical elements is of course going to be difficult, but there are a couple of interesting observations to be made in comparing the material elements with their non-material counterparts. Timothy Leary, who developed the 8-Circuit Model of Consciousness, later began to attempt to correlate this with the periodic table. Most scientists work with nine families of elements, but Leary opted for eight: Alkalis, Alkalines, Borons, Carbons, Nitrogens, Oxygens, Halogens and Noble Gases. The first four families, Leary argues, are terrestrial – they are heavy and tend to fall to Earth. The second four families are extraterrestrial – they tend to float off into space. In a similar fashion, he argues, the first four circuits of the nervous system are terrestrial; their function is to control survival and reproduction at the bottom of the 4,000-mile gravity well in which we presently live. The second four circuits are extraterrestrial – they will come into full play only when we live normally in zero-gravity – in free space. I'm not sure humans will ever live in zero-gravity, but through the integration of the spiritual counterparts of these last four families of elements – which we would attribute to the upper fifteen Aethyrs – we can perhaps strive to free our consciousness from its normal 'gravitational' constraints. This use of element families would seem to be an alternative approach of mapping the physical to spiritual elements.

Leary was not unique in dividing the elements into 8 families. In the 1860s English chemist John Newland purported to show that the elements are so arranged. In the 1870s, and with much more detail, Russian chemist Mendeleyev proved the validity of the eight family model; it is only in recent years that the nine family model has been adopted.

The number eight and the concept of periodicity are both relevant to Enochian magick, and to understand their importance it is instructive to consider the Law of Octaves. Scientist John Newland noticed that if each of the elements is arranged according to atomic weight, those with similar properties occur after each interval of seven elements, in a manner analogous to that in which the eighth note on a musical scale resembles the first note. Although John Newland's model has defects, it represented the first recognition of periodicity in the elements. So how can we apply the significance of the number 8 and Law of Octaves to Enochian magick? Well, quite startlingly, if we take the number of squares in the four Elemental Tablets (624), and divide by 8, we get 78, the number of cards in a Tarot deck. The Tarot is said to represent the Universe in all its possible facets of manifestation, so the 8 x 78 formula can be said be represent the Universe in all octaves, or modes of existence. 624 also seems to have a strong link with time, being 12 x 52, the number of months in a year multiplied by the number of weeks in a year. 624 is also 156 (the number of Babalon) multiplied by 4. Babalon (matter) as manifested through the four elements would seem one very obvious interpretation.

A periodicity based on the number 8 is evident in something of such integral importance to everyday life as the length of a week. Counting from say, Monday (and including Monday), it is eight places to the next Monday. Seven days in a week, but a periodicity of 8 between repeating days. One way in which periodicity can be seen to manifest in Enochian magick is through the mapping of the Aethyrs to the Sephiroth in the manner outlined previously, where, for example, BAG is mapped to Hod on an astral Tree of Life, ZEN to Hod on a mental Tree of Life and ZID to Hod on a spiritual Tree of Life. In this way we can see periodicity manifested through similarities between these three Aethyrs, with each exhibiting similar characteristics, though manifested in a progressively more abstract manner.

There is a secret contained in 624 that is alluded to in the Hebrew phrase that corresponds with it gematriacally, שאר זועם, which means 'the defence of the head, or helmet', and which was revealed to me through the 'chorkle' mentioned in Chapter One. Recall that chorkles are pointers relating to Enochian magick, which manifest in the form of something that is light blue in colour, and that the one in question was the traffic sign that indicates a no-through-road, taking the form of a headless cross in white against a light blue background. Confirmation of the significance of this chorkle seemed evident in the diary entry of the suicide whose books I had bought, who had written about a vision in which a leaf, sucked up into the atmosphere, had later fallen to ground in a T-shaped wheat field.

A powerful indication of the chorkle's importance came following my scrying of the 12th Aethyr, UTA. In my vision I found myself being nailed to a cross by a group of angelic beings. Mercifully, I felt no pain as the nails were being driven into my hands and feet, and even experienced a sense of exhilaration as the cross was lifted up by the entities, who then carried me on their shoulders to the place where I was to be crucified. This spot was a low hill, reminiscent of the place Jesus was put to death as depicted in films – apart from the climate, that is, which was temperate. As I hung on the cross, looking out over green fields that for some reason reminded me of the West Country, I saw in the distance a flash of white. As I continued to look, I observed that what I had seen was a white dove, and that it was flying toward me. When it reached me it perched on the cross, and began to peck at the 'head' of the cross – the small upright section that my head rested against. I experienced a great sense of love with the arrival of the bird; I became aware that the dove would stay with me for as long as I remained on the cross. The bird pecked furiously, until it had removed the 'head' of the cross.

The vision changed at this point, but it was this segment of it that kept replaying in my mind for days afterwards. There were two ways in which I could tie this imagery into the maps I use for the Aethyrs. Firstly, as a vision that occurred whilst exploring an Aethyr attributed to Chesed, it seemed quite apt that the dove showed 'mercy' to me in staying with me whilst I hung. Also, the cube – the geometrical shape attributed to Chesed – can be folded out to form the shape of a cross. I've certainly never suffered from any delusions of divinity, or notions that my path in life has very much in common with that of Christ! Then one day as I was looking at the Great Table I noticed afresh the 16 Calvary Crosses – four in each Elemental Tablet – and my heart leapt. The chorkle I had witnessed previously had been of a 'T' shape, or a regular cross with the top portion removed – the very section that the dove had been pecking at in my vision. It is certainly interesting that they are referred to as *Calvary* Crosses. I wondered if the letter occupying the square that forms the tops of these crosses might spell out an instruction, or the name of a hitherto unknown King or Angel. Jotting them down in the order they appear if reading from left to right seemed to produce nothing but gibberish; it forms the following sequence: i, l, a, a, a, a, c, s, n, v, o, n, u, r, m, i. Although I didn't seem any closer to a breakthrough in my search for a solution to this riddle, I remained convinced that there had to be one. My dreams continually took me back to my crucifixion during my exploration of UTA, and then I began to have dreams of witnessing Jesus' crucifixion, as well. These dreams always ended with Jesus' eyes being pecked out by a bird. I found this last detail puzzling, as it obviously differs from the Biblical account of what happened. On mentioning this dream to a friend, however, he informed me that in the film 'The Passion', directed by Mel Gibson, one of the thieves hung along with Jesus has his eyes pecked out by a crow! Still I couldn't make sense of the letters, and was about to give up on the whole idea of them having any significance, when one day I decided to put them into an anagram solver. I limited the anagram solutions to those containing a maximum of two words. I knew there wouldn't be a single word solution, but if I allowed solutions of more than two words I would end up with an output of thousands of meaningless phrases. And the result? There were two: aramaic nonvisual and narcomania visual! The first result struck me as being outstanding, when considered in the context of crosses and crucifixion. Jesus spoke Aramaic, and I had been having dreams about a Jesus who had his eyes pecked out whilst on the cross – one way of rendering the last few minutes of his life distinctly nonvisual! There was a marvellous synchronicity in the extraction of the word 'narcomaniac', as the previous night I had been watching a documentary about people who abuse painkillers, and had encountered the word narcomaniac (person who is hooked to one or more drugs) for the first time. This I took to be the Universe confirming that I was looking in the right direction.

We have to also consider that a headless cross – the idea that first sparked this chain of thought and discovery – is otherwise known as a Tau cross. Tau is of course the Hebrew letter for 'T', and Hebrew is the language that became corrupted into Aramaic. The letter tau is ascribed to the 32nd path of the Tree of Life. Could this fact shed any light on the significance of the headless cross in the context of the Great Table? I believe it does. My contention is that the Great Table represents a spiritual map *that reflects the material constituents of our physical universe.* As Above, So Below. The 32nd path of the Tree of Life corresponds to the card entitled 'The Universe' and relates to the transcendence of matter as part of the beginning of the spiritual journey. In reaching for the heavens we are forced to remember that our journey starts with the physical plane. Jesus' death on the cross, when seen in this light, can be viewed not so much as a means of absolving humanity of its sins, and more as a victory over materiality and its limitations.

In this discussion of missing heads, it is significant that the Bornless Ritual, used as a preliminary invocation in many Goetic workings, and also by Crowley as part of his technique for contacting one's Holy Guardian Angel (see Liber Samekh), was originally entitled the 'Headless Ritual'. This dates back to the ritual's origins in Ancient Egypt, where it was originally used as a method of exorcism. Headlessness might be thought to be a bad thing, but from the point of view of switching off the rational mind (which can interfere with gnostic insight), we need to temper our associations of negativity. Certainly, the rational mind can be a stumbling block in opening up a dialogue with one's Holy Guardian Angel. And how does all this relate to the Great Table? Well, both the knowledge and conversation of the Holy Guardian Angel and an absorption of the transformative powers of The Great Table would seem to represent the highest forms of personal alchemy, and a means of accessing the spiritual by mastery of the material.

Whilst discussing Tau crosses, it is worth noting that this

shape forms an important part of Crowley's ritual framework, with the Tau Cross of the Sephiroth surrounded by a circle representing for him the symbol of the Rose and Cross. The phallic imagery in a Tau cross is fairly obvious, as is the symbolic representation of the yoni by the circle. In my vision involving a Tau cross embedded in the earth, was I being shown 'materiality being fucked', as a means to its transcendence?

Intriguingly, some scholars are of the opinion that the cross Jesus was crucified on *was* a Tau cross. I came across this theory whilst reading 'The Secret Legacy of Jesus' by Jeffrey J. Butz. When, during my scrying session, I saw a bird pecking at the top of the Cross of Calvary, was I gaining a glimpse of the actual historical events of Jesus' death?

The Tau cross makes an appearance in the acronym for the O.T.O. – the Ordo Templi Orientis. Given the Order's emphasis on sex magick, the abbreviation's similarity to a penis flanked by two testicles is perhaps no coincidence. For those who have less sympathy for this magickal group, it could be argued that the acronym looks like two eyes, with a penis protruding from between them – dickheads!

The Tau cross is also present in the Angelic Seal of the Elemental Tablet of Air, where it appears with what looks very much like four Hebrew Yods above its cross-bar. Now get this. If we take the value of the Hebrew word 'tau' (400) and add it to the combined value of four Yods, we get 440. 440 equals the Hebrew for 'place of olives' (think Gethsemane), 'to be high' (which you tend to be on a cross), bitter things (Jesus was given vinegar to drink whilst on the cross), a dying person, and death generally. Just to compound this weirdness, if you add the value of all the numbers that ring the Sigillum dei Aemeth, you also get 440!

It is worth also considering the truncated pyramid – of significance in modern Enochian magic – as being analogous in some ways to the headless cross. Both the pyramids of Giza and the Cross of Calvary are considered symbols of eternal life – the cross by symbolising Jesus' return to life and the promise of heaven for believers, and the pyramid by being the 'machine' that propelled pharaohs into the afterlife. The Golden Dawn added truncated pyramids to each square of The Great Table so that their elemental forces could be more easily visualised. Interestingly, the placement of six truncated pyramids together creates a smaller cube within a larger one, and the shape known as the hypercube. The hypercube is the analogue of a fourth-dimensional cube, and as such is a very obvious pointer toward spirituality. This form even has thirty-two edges, one for each path of the Tree of Life!

What does all this discussion of crosses and crucifixion signify? I can only speculate – more research into the subject is needed – but my initial thoughts are that it has something to do with a theme running through Dee's contact with the Angels, and Enochian magick generally, which involves the wrenching pain we must all experience in turning our backs on the material in the pursuit of the spiritual. I am reminded of The Forty-Eighth Call, used to access the Aethyrs when scrying, which includes the following cheery message:

'. . . the Earth, let her be governed by her parts, and let there be division in her, that the glory of her may be always drunken and vexed in itself; her course, let it run with the heavens, and as a handmaid let her serve them; one season, let it confound another, and let there be no creature upon or within her the same; all her members let them differ in their qualities, and let there be no creature equal with another; the reasonable creatures of Earth (or men), let them vex and weed out one another; and the dwelling places, let them forget their names; the work of man and his pomp, let them be defaced; her buildings, let them become caves for the beasts of the field; confound her understanding with darkness. For why? It repenteth me I made man . . .'

The message in this passage seems to be that our material existence on earth is flawed by division and variety. We obsess about 'things' and the difference between different 'things', forgetting as we do so about the essential unity inherent in spirituality.

Whatever one thinks of the Christian message as it is commonly presented, the myth of Jesus as son of God is a powerful one. He incarnated as a regular man, tasted the pain of materiality and duality, and in being killed by ignorant, brutal humans, was liberated from the suffering he experienced whilst in a physical body.

There is another way in which Dee's revelations have their counterpart in the physical sciences, though this time it is Quantum Physics, not Chemistry, that gets the spotlight. Whilst reading Donald Tyson's 'Enochian magick for Beginners', I came across Appendix B, entitled 'The Vision Of The Round House', which is a transcript of a conversation that took place between Dee and Kelley in 1585, in which Kelley describes a vision he has received of a 'round house'. Said dwelling has four doors, corresponding to the four cardinal points of the compass, with each door also being assigned an element (the West door corresponds to Water, etc.). Kelley's visions corresponding to Water, Air and Fire took the form of dynamic flows of these elements, and Tyson produces diagrams to illustrate the form these took. I began reading this chapter just after spending a few hours with a Quantum Physics primer, and my first thought when I saw these diagrams was, *They look familiar!*

The concept from Quantum Physics that I was being reminded of by Tyson's diagrams were probability density plots corresponding to the wavefunctions of an electron in a hydrogen atom. The shape of the diagrammatic representation of the wavefunction varies depending on the values of three principal quantum numbers, but in many cases there is an uncanny similarity between them and the Currents of Water and Fire in the Round House. I'm not for a second suggesting that the Enochian angels were giving Dee hints to the underlying nature of physical reality – more that the essential nature of their spiritual vision is such that when represented graphically it shadows the essential nature of matter.

These revelations, and my regular scrying of the Aethyrs, eventually began to take their toll on me emotionally. I had yet to learn the importance of self-pacing when it comes to spiritual matters. Having scryed the first fifteen Aethyrs, with intervals of at least a week between each, I began to tackle consecutive Aethyrs on consecutive days, finishing my initial scrying of each level in just over two weeks. Like a good book that you want to read in one sitting, I was having so much fun with my exploration of the Aethyrs that I couldn't wait to move on the next one. I was finding progressive Aethyrs more 'entertaining' and vivid, which added to the compulsion to continue my astral journeying with minimum delay.

By the time I reached MAZ, the 6th Aethyr, I was becoming emotionally ragged. I didn't realise this at the time, so immersed was I in this other world I had discovered, but in hindsight this was definitely the case. By the time I reached the 4th Aethyr, PAZ, my waking consciousness started to overlap with the realm of the Aethyrs. I would often suddenly see the face of a character I had met during my scrying sessions, transposed onto the face of someone I was conversing with. At about the same time I began to experience poltergeist-like activity, especially in the morning. Alone in my house I would hear strange knocks. The television switched channels without my hand going near the remote. The strongest example of poltergeist activity was the classic moving furniture scenario. On two occasions the same dining room chair moved backwards from the table, as if an invisible diner was excusing himself from the table.

After I had completed my initial scrying of each of the Aethyrs I wanted to start all over again. And I would have, were it not for a dream I had in which an angelic being I took to be Ave firmly instructed me not to. Whether it was really Ave that appeared to me, or just my subconscious giving me a needed steer, when I woke up I decided I would take a break. A second after I made this decision there was a terrific crashing sound from the living room. Running through to see what had happened, I got chills up my spine as I saw that the black bowl I had used to keep sifted sand in all those years before lying smashed on the floor. Somehow, it had moved seven inches from its customary place on a side table, to topple to its destruction. If I'd had any remaining doubts about taking a rest from my scrying, this incident removed them immediately.

I was free from my obsession, but I knew there was one last thing I had to do before I could call it truly over. Quickly dressing, I grabbed a banana and left the house, buttoning my shirt as I marched to the tube station. Half an hour later I emerged at Covent Garden tube station, and walked quickly toward the British Museum. For the previous ten years I had known that the museum held Dee's wax Sigillum dei Aemeth and a couple of his scrying stones, and finally I was going to eyeball them. As it was fairly early on a Tuesday morning, the museum was quiet – just as I wanted it to be – and as I walked into the room that contained the Dee exhibits I was pleased to see that myself and an attendant were pretty much the only people present.

My heart raced as I saw the Dee items. They looked smaller than I had imagined they would – both the scrying stones and the Sigillum dei Aemeth – but what they lacked in physical size they more than made up for in pedigree. I couldn't get over the fact that I was staring at objects that both Dee and Kelly had held; that I was looking at stones through which angels had spoken. My concentration moved to the larger of the crystals; I felt compelled to stare into its depths. Minutes passed, and suddenly I realised that I was sufficiently altered to begin to scry. With a shiver of anticipation, I surrendered to this urge.

Scrying whilst standing would not generally be recommended, but the cumulative exhaustion of the previous weeks, combined with the fillip using Dee's stones provided, meant that I went into trance quite easily, quickly losing touch with my physical surroundings. I had never used a crystal to scry with before, but had no trouble immersing myself in its glassy depths. Soon I saw the outline of a door, as it might appear if standing in darkness and seeing light stream through the gap between door and frame from a lit room. I clasped the door's handle – a brass knob – and turned. Immediately the brilliance of the light emanating from the room hit me, causing momentary blindness. It was as if a thousand suns were burning just feet from my face. Slowly my vision improved, so that I was able to discern figures moving in the room. One individual stood quite close to me, and looking at him I instinctively knew it was the Angel Ave. 'His' face was androgynous but more male than female, had a bluish hint, and very beautiful. I opened my mouth to speak, but before any words could emerge the vision of Ave disappeared. Now I was looking at columns of numbers on a vast computer screen, all of them scrolling upwards at a terrific rate. I sensed huge data flows, as if I was tapping into a main trunk line of the World Wide Web. The numbers were a neon purple on a white background, and seemed to wink at me as they whizzed by. The vision changed and I was now looking at the figure of Christ on the cross. He looked like a traditional depiction of Jesus cruci-fied, except the same numerals were rushing across his body, like ants pouring over a corpse. Absurdly, I found myself won-dering whether this data stream would cause Christ to itch. At the foot of the cross I saw a mangy dog, and was astonished to see it urinating against the heavy wooden upright.

Suddenly everything went blank, and the next thing I knew I was lying on the floor, staring up at the ceiling. I got to my feet and looked around. No-one seemed to have noticed my collapse. Taking one last glance at Dee's magickal tools, I walked out of the room and then out of the museum.

CHAPTER ELEVEN

My scrying session at the British Museum ended my period of Dee mania. Which wasn't to say that my interest had gone; just that I allowed other things into my life apart from Enochian exploration – like sleeping and eating. It wasn't until I'd permitted a bit of sanity to return that I realised just how powerful my Dee obsession had become, and quite how strong the Aethyric scrying sessions I had undertaken had been. Looking back at my magickal record and comparing it to my 'ordinary' journal I could see that during my intensive period of scrying I had frequent bouts of illness. This time was also characterised by the occurrence of several mini-crises – life-lessons that forced me to confront hitherto unacknowledged sides of my character.

It has often been said that the angels of the Enochian system are actually alien entities, and I would have to say that I accept that this might be true. My support for this notion is based on the entities I have encountered whilst scrying the Aethyrs, which often took the shape of insectoid aliens, without any parallel to anything that might be found on Earth. Of course, when I talk of alien entities, I don't for a second think that they travel from Mars to hang out with scryers; I think more likely they are from parallel universes or dimensions and have nothing directly to do with anything that emanated from our own Big Bang. I mention this because I think it may explain the strong effects that many report after an Enochian working. The contact is often so strong and so unlike anything we are used to that to afterwards feel drained is probably quite natural. The blurring of the alien and the spiritual is a constant theme throughout metaphysics, though figuring out where, if at all, there is a legitimate overlap seems a very difficult task. Certainly some evidence seems to suggest that certain people make sense of spiritual experiences such as astral projection by means of the alien abduction hypothesis, 'fitting' their memories of what happened to match accounts they have read or heard about. There is of course the possibility that we humans are just pets being kept by a vastly superior race, with traits akin to those we ascribe to God, and that every supernatural experience we humans have is just us taking a step closer to that ultimate truth!

My unbalanced reaction to my Enochian odyssey led me to consider my own imperfect state, and I was eager to examine and diagnose the shortcomings which had been highlighted by my Aethyric explorations. I see Aethyric journeying as akin to dropping depth charges into one's subconscious; sometimes they explode quickly, and we get a strong reaction we immediately associate with the ritual, but very often there is a lengthy lag time between working and 'detonation', with the effects being delayed but far-reaching.

At this stage in my life the experiences I had had in facing my demons had centred around Evangelical Christianity and Modern Western Psychotherapy, both of which I felt had huge shortcomings in dealing with the human condition (as well as strengths – I have to concede that). Christianity I had the least time for; its central tenet that we are all born sinners and need salvation to right this condition is obviously both wrong and mentally damaging to anyone who accepts it unquestioningly. Psychotherapy, for all its complex models and theories, seems to fail in the one area that we'd all like to see it succeed: getting results. People taking part in talking therapies seem to get better in spite of their treatment; other events and the passage of time seem to have more of an effect in bringing about a 'cure'.

My thoughts eventually turned to the Goetic demons of the Lesser Key of Solomon as a means of really grappling with my shadow side. I was also intrigued to see whether I could confound my scepticism and evoke a demon to visible appearance. It seemed a great way of laying to rest (in my own mind at least) the debate about whether or not this is possible. At this stage I *still* wasn't sure whether demons should be viewed as an objectification of a psychological or spiritual principle, or as identities that can be considered to have an external, objective reality. My reasoning was that either way, to summon such a spirit would be a means of reconciling in myself the quality it represented. I was at the time aware of having a huge amount of anger – anger whose source was in some ways a mystery to me, and which I struggled to direct constructively. I thought that if I could raise a demon that had anger and wrath as one of its defining features, I could learn how to direct *my* own anger and wrath. The Goetic demons are most commonly evoked in order to carry out a specific, material request, and this was certainly not the case as far as I was concerned. I wasn't after money, love or revenge. It was more of an alchemical quest that I was on.

The first task that I was presented with was assembling the necessary ritual tools and supplies. Despite a magickal career that had spanned almost twenty years, I was astonished to realise how little I had in the way of magickal paraphernalia. I think a couple of incense burners and a long quartz crystal was about all I had in my ritual armoury. I don't subscribe to the belief that if the altar cloth is the wrong colour, or if the wand is an inch too short and made of the wrong wood, then a ritual is doomed to failure. Nevertheless, I felt it necessary to be in as comfortable a psychological space as possible prior to the evocation, and I considered spending some time acquiring ritual tools an important part of this process.

As I hadn't gone to the effort of forging my own sword, and cutting a sapling to fashion into a wand, I felt it right to put a good deal of effort into the consecration of my ritual tools. I have always liked the smell of Abramelin Oil and Incense (Crowley variety) – I think it's the cinnamon – and decided to make my own Abramelin Oil to use in my consecration ceremony. Its ingredients are cinnamon, myrrh and galangal essential oils, along with olive oil. The cinnamon and myrrh were available from a local New Age store, but the galangal seemed impossible to track down – before I looked on the Internet. Eventually I ordered everything apart from the olive oil on the Internet, along with pipettes and empty bottles. I used the pipettes to drop the right proportions into a beaker, and then mixed and poured the contents into empty bottles. Voila! Strange though this may sound, with the mixing of the oils, I had begun my Goetic evocation. No, I mean that. I could go further and say that with my decision to undertake the evocation the ritual had began. As soon as our conscious and unconscious minds acknowledge a forthcoming ritual, they start to prepare for the working. I have often noticed myself slipping into an altered state of consciousness as I begin to clean my temple on the morning of a ritual, for example. When this happens it is often a sign that I am ready for the work ahead, and that the ritual is going to be successful.

The next step was to decide on a demon to evoke, and this involved much research and meditation. All of which I then promptly ignored. Instead I decided to allow the Universe decide which demon I would invoke, on the assumption that it probably knew better than me. With 72 demons in the Goetia, each is said to rule 5 days of the year. I simply chose a Saturday about four weeks distant which I knew would work for me; I would evoke whichever demon ruled that particular day. As soon as I made this decision I had a moment of misgiving. What if I got a real badass demon? Nevertheless, I stuck to my plan, and the demon that I ended up getting in my lottery was Malthus.

I wanted to do all I could do to ensure the success of my evocation. To this end, in the week leading up to the ritual I put myself through a series of exercises and observances aimed at cleansing and exhausting myself, as well as generating as high a psychic 'charge' as possible. I haven't eaten any meat other than fish for years, but I went totally vegetarian. I limited myself to three hours sleep a night. I increased my daily exercise from half an hour to an hour and a half. In an attempt to overwhelm my rational mind I employed a variety of tricks. I gave all of my friends and family Hindu names, which, much to their annoyance, I used to address them. My son Alex became Jagdish, I

recall. I spent an hour a day focusing on conflicting concepts
– life and death, fear and peace, wealth and poverty, etc. I also
spent half an hour a day practising Austin Osmond Spare's
'Death Posture'. The mind-blowing experience I'd had with a
mirror whilst a student encouraged me to try this technique as
a means of entering a state a gnosis, and it didn't disappoint. I
knocked a few bolts out of the girders of my mind through this
means.

In the build-up to the evocation working a number of synchronicities occurred which persuaded me that the Universe was
behind me in my actions. When opening a book to find out
which Goetic demon ruled the period during which I would be
performing the ritual, the book fell open to exactly the right
page. I had been worried about setting off smoke alarms and
generally attracting unwanted attention through performing my
evocation, when it occurred to me that on the Friday before the
weekend I had earmarked for my working I was due to commence the lease on a new shop, said shop to be handed over to
me in shell condition – bare concrete floors, white painted walls
and ceiling, and pretty much nothing else. A perfect setting for
the evocation; as the shop would later be painted and carpeted
I could even paint straight onto the floors and walls! Furthermore, the shop's street number was '72', exactly the same as the
number of Goetic demons!

It occurred to me that in using Goetic magick to reconcile
my warring sub-personalities that I was attempting something
similar to the pursuit of the knowledge and conversation of
my Holy Guardian Angel, a task famously covered in 'The
Sacred Magic of Abramelin the Mage'. I think it's important
to remember that Western Ceremonial Magicians don't have a
monopoly on a relationship with their daemon, even if they are
the chief group who conceptualise their higher self thus. Being
filled with the spirit, achieving self-realisation, experiencing a
kundalini rising episode, attaining enlightenment – these are all
experiences that, if not entirely identical to it, share many similarities with opening up a dialogue with one's Holy Guardian
Angel. I think there has been a tendency amongst many spiritual

writers to obfuscate and mystify what is actually a very natural human aspiration. I'm actually with the Born Again Christians in having the courage to claim spiritual victory by proclaiming themselves saved, rather than expecting to sit through hours of church and prayer before daring to hope for eternal life. Incidentally, I don't believe the Christian dogma of Original Sin, and any of the other bunkum about a Second Coming, Heaven and Hell, etc., but I am aware that there are Christians, who though they wouldn't conceptualise it as such, have come to enjoy a deep and nurturing relationship with their Higher Self/Holy Guardian Angel/Call Him What Thou Wilt through prolonged prayer, meditation and concentration on the needs of others. The roads are many, the destination the same. The important thing is to begin the journey with the expectation of reaching your destination, but in the knowledge that even if you don't (in this incarnation), your life will have been immeasurably enriched by making the attempt. Do What Thou Wilt is a call for every soul to undertake the pursuit of self-knowledge and spiritual berthing, though each man and woman has a different path to follow. Much sadness may be experienced along the way, but in the context of a spiritual journey we are capable of accepting this.

I intended to follow the format of Aleister Crowley's Goetia in approaching my evocation of demons, though omitting the Enochian calls, which seemed to me to just be tacked on as an afterthought as a means of bolstering the ritual. Why Crowley thought that using an angelic language to evoke demons was a good idea I can't really think. Incidentally, the use of the Rite of the Bornless One as the preamble to Aleister Crowley's Goetia is also quite odd, in that it is actually an ancient Egyptian exorcism, but I was happy to retain this element of the ritual, as the use of the juxtaposition of opposites fits with my notions of creating psychic tension as a means to enabling evocation.

Discussion of the inclusion of seemingly antagonistic ritual elements (such as a prayer of exorcism) in an evocation of demons leads us to ponder what exactly we are doing when we perform a ritual, especially as regards the words that are spoken. I'm reminded of words like abracadabra, which as children we learnt could open treasure chests and locked doors. Are we to believe that words have intrinsic power, which when used in a working have the ability to call forth demons, or is it the arrangement of words and actions that somehow triggers a change in ourselves, which alters our state of consciousness, thereby enabling us to perceive things we previously couldn't? I think ritual words only have significance numerologically and gematriacally, except in as much as their proper vibration can cause changes in the environment and consciousness (but in the latter case this is due to sound waves not the meaning of the words per se). I believe the majority of the power of ritual words stems from the meaning it conveys to the subconscious, and from this point of view a Goetic evocation could incorporate the words bubblegum and candyfloss if these words somehow triggered the right chord in the magician.

This brings us to the realisation that ritual is just a prop, a means of bootstrapping our magickal personality. The highest adepts can work their magick with nothing more than the power of Will – words, candles and daggers are totally superfluous to them. Which isn't to say they aren't important to the rest of us, but I think if we bear in mind that ritual is a means to an end, and not the end itself, we'll be less frightened of not slavishly following the ritual formats of others. The idea that a Goetic demon isn't going to show up because there has been a slight error in the drawing of his sigil is just plain ridiculous, though a misconception a lot of magicians have. Whenever I consider this notion I get the mental picture of a hideous demon, standing off-stage in a theatre with arms crossed and scowl on his face, refusing to go on to deliver his part because another actor has mispronounced his name.

Just as ritual words and paraphernalia don't make a magickal act, so occult orders that like to dress up in their robes every other Saturday and wave their arms around should not fool themselves into thinking they are necessarily doing anything magickal. My experience of a number of magickal orders has led me to believe that many of them are nothing more than amateur dramatics groups, with degrees and emblems bolted on to persuade the deluded that they are treading a spiritual path. When a maladjusted twenty-eight-year-old who lives at home with his mother and has an obsession with computer games informs you that he is a Great Hierophant of the Order of the Golden Cross, you have to wonder whether something has gone badly wrong with his grasp on reality. Magick involves directly experiencing and influencing the finer planes – astral, mental and spiritual – and anything else, however elegantly it is dressed up, is not magick.

Back to my Goetic evocation. Eventually the appointed afternoon arrived, and I was ready to meet Malthus, an Earl of Hell, who commands 26 legions of demons and 'builds towers and fills them with ammunition and weapons'. (The thought crossed my mind that the Ministry of Defence should really hear about this chap, but I've yet to draw their attention to him.) Preparing my temple (the shop) took a fair while, as after giving it a thorough clean I had to set up an altar, the circle and Triangle of Art. Talismans and magickal weapons had to be laid out, my incense brazier prepared, and candles arranged. I had constructed a Hexagram and Pentagram of Solomon, and a Ring of Solomon, by photocopying examples of them, which I then laminated and chopped to size. I was going to burn the Incense of Abramelin I had made using a charcoal brazier (purchased from a website that specialises in supplying Catholic churches). I thought about performing the evocation in the nude, but I eventually opted to wear my black magickal robe.

Eventually all was done, and I was ready to begin. I meditated for about twenty minutes to try and get myself into what I considered to be the optimal mental state, before conducting a Lesser Banishing Ritual and Crowley's Star Ruby. I don't feel it's necessary to commit every part of a ritual to memory, but I knew by heart both of these rituals, along with the Bornless Rite.

I think the first seeds of doubt emerged even as I was performing my banishings. I just didn't *feel* like anything was going to happen. The feeling grew throughout my recitation of the evocation, so that by the time I got to the conjuration, I *knew* I wasn't going to see or sense Malphus. And so, I guess it came as no great surprise when that is exactly what happened. I have to say, I felt particularly ridiculous standing robed in my magickal circle, listening to the sound of traffic go by outside. I felt unmasked as a little boy who refused to grow up, clinging instead to notions of demons and magick spells.

I was so disheartened I almost didn't bother to banish before leaving the circle, but I went through the motions anyway. Tidying up my magickal paraphernalia, I resolved to spend the evening watching mindless television, and not to devote any time to magickal books or practices for at least a week. Feeling as I did, I wasn't sure I'd *ever* go back to them. Despite the promise I had made to myself, I couldn't stop myself from conducting a post-mortem on my attempted evocation as I watched rubbish on television. What had I done wrong? Was I deluding myself in thinking that spirits existed? Was the whole of the occult nothing more than wishful thinking and a flight from reality? Just when I was on the point of deciding it *was* all a waste of time, the memory of my experiences in Africa returned. There was no way *they* had been imagined. Thinking of these events reminded me of the many other mystico-magickal experiences I had had. I was comforted by the knowledge that there *were* supernatural dimensions. What's more, a key feature in the experiences I had had was that many were unsought. Was there something I could learn from this fact?

This led me to consider the nature of anticipation. What exactly is it, and how can it interfere with spiritual practices? The first thought I had was that anticipation is being somewhere other than 'here and now'. It's projecting your consciousness away from the present moment. Living in the present is something that is stressed as being of great importance for those wanting to grow spiritually, and a sign that one *is* growing spiritually, so from this point of view the state of anticipation struck me as being less than ideal when it comes to doing magick. Anticipation – for most people at least – involves visualisation. We imagine what is going to be happening at some point in the future. It was apparent to me as soon as I considered this that my suspicion that I wasn't going to succeed in evoking a demon had immediately translated into a vivid picture of what did in fact transpire – myself standing in a circle, staring at an empty Triangle of Art. I was in effect doing magick to stop my magick working – and it worked!

So how to solve this problem? I considered getting whacked out of my head on drugs, but although I believe mind-altering substances have their place in spiritual practices, I considered Goetic demons – if I could get one to turn up – to be a little too wily to be dealt with in a less than sharp frame of mind. There was also the matter of wanting to explore the extent of demons' objective reality, and the problem of trying to do this when drugs are mixing up my objective and subjective realities.

A useful take on things occurred to me whilst looking at a rainbow, about a week after my first unsuccessful attempt at a Goetic evocation. In considering whether demons exist, it seemed unlikely that whichever Supreme Being is behind our universe had devised seventy-two nasties to add to the mix to simply 'liven things up'. If demons exist, they must exist as manifestations of unbalanced force, and just as white light is comprised of the full spectrum of colours, so 'evil' could be seen to be a composite of each of the seventy-two impulses represented by the Goetic demons. Since their identification, magicians' discussion and conjuration of these demons has fleshed them out on the astral plane, giving them the appearance they have historically taken. This conceptualisation of matters helped me, as it enabled me to see the Goetic demons as 'real', without having to believe a naïve and simplistic theory as to how they came to be.

Armed with an intellectually acceptable theory of the origin of demons, the next challenge was to get one to show up in a way which fulfilled the definition of evocation. It didn't have to punch a hole in my ceiling making its appearance, by I wanted to be able to detect the critter at least astrally, and to be able to charge it with carrying out the task I had in mind for it. It still seemed to me that contrast was the key to this – the juxtaposition of opposites creating a 'charge' or 'current' which would power the manifestation I desired, but I felt I needed to utilise this concept more pro-actively.

Those familiar with Dion Fortune's writings about the 'Circuit of Force', or those who have paid attention to the dynamic of the first three Sephiroth of the Tree of Life – indeed, those who have looked at Hegel's treatment of dialectics – should readily grasp what I mean by using the juxtaposition of opposites to create. It is no accident that the target demon is instructed to appear in the *Triangle* of Art, this shape's apex representing the resolution of two opposing forces.

How does this all work in practice? Well, in the case of the summoning of a demon, we have to take the desired outcome (the demon present in our triangle, communicating with the magus) and ask ourselves, which two polar opposite states would this result equilibrate? A condition in which the demon stalks the magus (or joins him in the circle) and the condition of the demon never showing itself (perhaps not even existing) would be 'balanced' by the entity appearing in the triangle. The trick is to hold both extreme and unwanted states in mind simultaneously, a circuit thereby being created which will exist until it is resolved by the demon appearing in the triangle. In the case of a ritual of evocation, the time to carry out this visualisation exercise would be just before the official summoning of the demon.

Now there's more. Depending on your ability to visualise, you may need to turbo-charge your ritual to succeed in manifesting the demon, and this is best done using sex-magick. If you are carrying out the ritual alone, your choice as to how you go about this will be limited, but if this is the case, don't worry! Trying to work sex-magick with a partner is not without its distractions and problems, so that in some ways auto-erotic techniques are more straightforward. Do I need to spell it out? Okay, if you insist. Whilst holding the images of the two extreme situations that are to be equilibrated by the appearance of the demon in the triangle, masturbate. Sexualising the image of the two (unwanted) extremes will help to maintain an erotic charge. The demon that has entered your circle could be highly attractive and trying to rape you, and the image of a non-existent demon could involve an empty room in a brothel, with a porno film showing on a television in the background. You don't want to make these polar opposite images too enticing, but just enough to get those sexual energies flowing.

If the circuit of force technique with sexual energies doesn't work, you can add drugs. If *this* doesn't work, you are not cut-out for magick, have the psychic sensitivity of pumpkin, and should probably consider a career in banking.

Returning briefly to the fruitful comparison between magick and chemistry's periodic table, it is interesting to note the discovery of 'triads' by chemists who were pioneers in discovering the relationship between the elements. In essence, it was found that in some cases the atomic weights of three similar elements was such that the average of two equalled the third. Almost as if the two were exuding or pushing out the third in a manner analogous to the circuit of force!

Three weeks after my initial failure with Goetic evocation, I tried again, this time using the circuit of force technique. My target demon was Bifrons, and the operation was a total success. As I held in my mind the two opposing images designed to emanate my target demon, I started to get an electrical buzzing sensation in my temple, and I felt like a radio tuner that was scanning the full spectrum of frequencies. Within a few seconds there was a 'lock-on' and I had the unmistakeable impression of connecting strongly with the demon. There was an absolute certainty that this contact was genuine – not an ounce of doubt that I was kidding myself or the victim of wishful thinking. I was looking at the Triangle of Art at this stage, and there seemed to be a shimmering effect taking place involving the incense smoke that was wafting up, but the contact also involved a hard-to-describe 'knowing' or gnosis, followed by mental pictures – psychic flashes if you will – of the demon. He looked fairly grotesque, and not totally dissimilar to the 'artists' impressions' of him I had previously seen.

Bifron shape-shifted at one point, to appear to me in the

shape of a two-headed hunchback. His heads were on quite long necks, and each shifted and swivelled constantly like writhing snakes. We communicated telepathically, with his right head seeming to 'send' harsher messages than his left. I didn't want Bifrons to find me treasures, or deliver unto me a fair maiden – I was interested in integrating in myself the unbalanced traits he represents. I conveyed this request verbally – the demon was charged to balance the unbalanced force he signifies in my own psyche. No sooner had this demand been made, than the two heads of Bifrons took on huge significance for me. The thought 'I'm two-faced' came to me, and I had to concede that there were times when I thought one thing and said another. I didn't have to wrestle Bifrons to the ground to feel the full impact of this lesson. The realisation came quickly and painlessly. Just before the 'Licence to Depart' I got an overpowering whiff of stale sweat and tobacco. I assume this smell was Bifrons', as I had recently bathed, and don't smoke. The banishing was accomplished successfully, and I was able to revel in the satisfaction of an instructive and successful evocation. I'd seen Bifrons – psychically – and he'd given me a valuable insight into my own psychological make-up.

Returning for a second to where my evocation rituals were being performed, the fact that the new shop allowed me to conduct my summoning on bare concrete is a point that would have been noted with approval by Joseph C. Lisiewski. In his book, 'Ceremonial Magick And The Power Of Evocation,' he presents his theories on the mechanics of, and requirements for, successful evocation, one of them being that the ceremony should be performed on, or as close as possible to, bare earth. He believes that the energies generated during a ritual need to be earthed for evocation to physical manifestation to occur successfully. While I am not sure just how relevant 'earthing' magickal energies is, it is interesting that this is an example of someone else borrowing concepts from science to make sense of the magickal. Not just that, but the similarity between electricity and magickal energies is being highlighted, something I certainly agree with.

The same author believes that something he terms a state of

'Subjective Synthesis' is essential to the manifestation to physical appearance of spirits. I think this is a good example of where the whole subjective/objective debate can get very tangled and twisted. Would a state of 'objective synthesis' help in the manifestation of spirits *psychologically*, for example? Let's get Lisiewski's definition of the subjective synthesis, which is a state produced 'through the conscious study, understanding, comprehension, and acceptance of the theory of all elements that compose a magical act. As a result of this synthesis, an integrated belief system is taken up by the Practitioner's subconscious mind. This allows the individual to perform the magic . . .'

What the author seems to be saying here is that if you brainwash yourself, you can make yourself believe that you've seen the physical manifestation of a spirit. I don't mean to be cynical, but I can't see how else to interpret the above. Why is a spirit going to care if you've conducted a 'subjective synthesis', unless the 'physical manifestation' is actually a subjective manifestation, reliant on your own mind, to occur? I agree that being in the right mental state is important for acts of evocation, but I don't agree that physical manifestation is wholly dependent on it – partly because I don't believe that full physical manifestation *ever* occurs, and partly because what physical effects may be evident can occur irrespective of the mental states of those present. Take the case of a poltergeist haunting, for example. It may be happening because of the mental and emotional state of its focus – often an adolescent girl – but that won't stop its physical effects (furniture moving, objects flying around) being apparent to whomever is present when it manifests.

Where are our modern-day demons? I was wondering a few weeks back. If they are real, then surely they are capable of making themselves heard and seen without the arduous efforts of magicians – there must be times when they erupt spontaneously onto the public domain. Perhaps this is what wars and famines represent, but surely demons don't always need to rely on disaster and bloodshed to show themselves? It was a couple of days after this thought that I passed an advertisement for a mobile phone company. They were using six 'made up' monsters to personify the six most common complaints customers have with their broadband Internet provider. As an example, there was a two-headed beast reminiscent of a primitive dinosaur that was termed a 'Crafty-Cost Nark', which was meant to be responsible for higher than necessary bills. In the pose in which the beast was represented, its two long necks form a 'V' sign, as if this might be the message some broadband companies are giving their customers, and the monster appears blind, pre-sumably mirroring the fact that some mobile companies don't see the annoyance their customers feel.

When the advertising people devised this campaign, the appearance of the 'monsters' was to a certain extent determined by the negative aspects of mobile phone companies they were trying to portray, but beyond this, the imaginations of the creatives involved were given full reign – and this would have been a group process, meaning aspects of the collective unconscious might be tapped into. Let's take another of the Internet beasts, the 'Mystery Speed Mook' and see what its appearance reveals. This critter is in the form of a four legged animal, with a hooded face, of which only its eyes are visible. Turning to the Lesser Key of Solomon, I quickly discovered that he bore a resemblance to Uvall, who has been variously depicted as a *four-legged* dromedary and a *hooded* man. The Mystery Speed Mook is meant to represent the tendency of some broadband companies to predict connection speeds that the majority of their customers do not end up enjoying. Interesting then that Uvall is said to 'know of the past and *future*!

It could be argued that a fictitious character that is meant to possess negative characteristics is likely to have something in common with one demon from a long and varied list of demons. But instead of saying this means the similarity proves *nothing*, we can instead say that this proves *everything*! The qualities represented by the demons are alive in this world, and manifest in a myriad of ways. Does this then mean that the demons are nothing more than personifications of universal qualities? I would say that the answer to this question is 'no'. They *are* personifications of universal qualities, but they also have the capacity to manifest in a manner that exhibits all the qualities of self-directed behaviour and a desire to carry out objectives that are inherent to their nature. How do they take this form? Through the utilisation of energy. Money can give them form, as in the case of the advertising campaign discussed, which certainly cost the company that commissioned it millions. Human energy is probably their most common power source, and this highlights the importance of sex-magick, as it is through sexuality that man can most readily tap vast quantities of bio-energetic power. Disasters, which typically involve the release of vast amounts of energy, can also give form to demons, both for those experiencing the disaster and for the descendants of those who experienced it, who will hear stories of the cataclysm – stories that will haunt their imaginations and dreams. I am reminded of the photograph of the cloud of debris as one of the United Airlines 737s crashed into the Twin Towers, which bore the image of a hideous face grimacing, almost as if the smoke and dust issuing from the struck building was being moulded by the hijackers' hatred.

CHAPTER TWELVE

So we now come to the 'tying it all together' section of the book. In the first chapter I indicated some of the questions I hoped to be able to answer in this modest tome, and now is the time to assess whether I have succeeded in this respect, and whether we can draw any conclusions as a result. Let's start with the primary question I raised, 'Do spirits have objective reality?'

I think the idea suggested in the first chapter, that perhaps this is the wrong question to ask, continues to apply after taking into account the experiences described in this book. The line of reasoning I used was that in a sense everything we perceive is 'subjective', as we can only perceive through our own eyes, the information from the world being represented in our own individual brain. I mentioned that advances in quantum mechanics raise questions as to how much we are perceivers of reality, and how much we are actually creators of reality. Consider my successful evocation of a Goetic spirit, and the technique used. In one sense my evocation method was an act of creation, using the circuit of force to manifest this entity.

Leaving philosophical questions aside, perhaps the question we should be asking is, 'Do spirits *behave* as if they have objective reality?' To this, I think the answer is certainly 'yes'. If the Magician has entered a sufficiently deep state of gnosis, Goetic spirits, Enochian angels, sprites and hobgoblins will all behave as if they are independent, self-willed, objective entities. Consider the spirit that attacked me whilst fishing in Africa, which was totally external to me and came unbidden to disturb my peace. The trick is knowing how to attain these states of gnosis, especially if you aren't naturally psychic, but pranayama and meditation, combined with the 'circuit-of-force' technique mentioned in the preceding chapter, should do the trick.

My research and experimentation has led me to the view that spirits do not manifest in a physical, flesh-and-blood form. I will change my mind on this matter as soon as someone demonstrates otherwise, but in the absence of such an exposition I remain confident of this assertion. The evocation of a spirit can, however, involve electromagnetic disturbances and the shifting of finer energies. 'Evocation of a demon to physi-cal appearance' may not happen, but 'evocation of a demon to clairvoyant appearance' is certainly possible. The ability of spirits to manipulate our physical world directly is for the most part limited, and to the extent that it has been demonstrated, appears to operate through the etheric energies of humans. Emotion, especially sexually charged emotion, is one of the more common 'fuels' for this etheric energy, and this explains the importance of sex magick, the drama of ritual, and the fact that adolescent girls are so often the focus for poltergeist behaviour. Just because spirits can't easily *directly* influence the physical world does not mean that magickal works involving the evocation of spirits are likely to be of limited potency. If we accept that magick typically works by manipulating the astral plane, with this in due course feeding down to the physical plane, then it becomes apparent that having a demon let off a few hand grenades on the astral plane will have a powerful, if indirect, influence on the material world.

I see spirits, be they Vodoun entities, Enochian angels, Goetic demons or leprechauns, as parts of our psyche in accord with the Hermetic maxim 'as above, so below' – in the same way that as part of Ultimate Oneness we each have a bit of everything else in us, and are each in everything else as well. At the same time, whilst these beings don't have a physical counterpart (as we conceive of it), on more refined levels of existence – the astral plane, for example – they seem to have what approximates to objective reality. 'Subjective-objective' reality would be a better term for their status on these planes. As an example, two people are capable of seeing the demon Bifrons in its astral form, but he may look slightly different to each. Reality seems to be a participative activity! If we imagine an equilateral triangle with the concepts of 'objective' and 'subjective' occupying the lower left and lower right points respectively, 'universality' would be the concept we would place at the apex of the triangle, the transcending idea that unites and negates the objective/subjective dichotomy. From this point of view we can argue that to worry about the objective reality of spirits is in some respects a meaningless task.

I devoted three chapters to my Enochian explorations. What conclusions would I draw in terms of the validity of Dee's magick? I know that without a doubt it 'works' – it does what it says on the can – and to paraphrase Crowley, 'if certain procedures are followed, certain results will follow'. Press the 'call' button and they will come! Without a time machine it is impossible for anyone alive now to verify beyond a shadow of a doubt what transpired between Dee and Kelly – whether there was any subterfuge or self-deception on the part of either – but the strength of the visions I received, their deep symbolic content, and the synchronicities and general weirdness that surrounded my Enochian adventures combine to make me believe that we can have faith in Enochian magick as true method of personal alchemy and spiritual advancement.

The strange thing is that, even if Dee and Kelly *were* both charlatans, it wouldn't necessarily invalidate their legacy, and this leads to my alternate theory of Enochian magick. Now watch this, I'm about to invent a new 'spiritual system'. One afternoon last summer, whilst on holiday in the Atlas mountains of Morocco, I fell into a swoon. I collapsed beneath a huge cypress tree, and had the most astounding waking dream. I found myself at the gates of a castle made entirely of ice. An angel of sublime beauty emerged from the castle, and came and placed his hands on my shoulders. Looking deep into my eyes he said, 'I am Galandrel. You have been chosen by the Creator to carry an important message to humanity. Come with me.'

Taking my hand he led me into the castle's courtyard. The early morning sun made the turrets of the castle glisten. In the centre of the courtyard was a fountain, the water from its jet frozen as it gushed upward to create the effect of looking at photograph of a normal fountain. On the far side of the courtyard was a turret that rose high above all the others; the windows at the top were tiny specks. The angel led me toward this structure.

On entering it I found myself standing in a vast lobby, the ceiling of which extended all the way to the top of the tower. Numerous floors were visible, extending upwards like donuts stacked on top of each other. A lift, opposite the entrance, allowed access to the various floors. Again, everything was made of what looked like ice.

The angel lifted his hand up and said, 'These are the twenty-one levels of experience and attainment. By experiencing each you will finally come to the top floor, Choralin, which equates to Unity with God.

'How do you get to the top?' I asked. 'How do I ride the lift?'

'That is the challenge that faces all of humanity,' the angel replied soberly. 'The colours of the floors will give you some idea. Now, I will take you to a floor of your choosing, then our time together is over.'

'Any floor?' I asked 'Even the top one?'

'Anyone but the top one.'

I opted for the Pink Level, thirteen floors up. It seemed like a safe compromise. After letting the angel know my choice, I was led over to one of the lifts, and shortly we began our ascent. I would describe the sights and sounds that followed, but this information is only available to initiates of my Order. Information on joining, including fees, at the rear of the book. Joke!

'But you've admitted none of this happened,' I hear you say, 'so why are you filling a couple of pages with this non-sense?' The reason I've included this section is because – well, because it works. See Appendix One for a full list of the levels 'revealed' to me, along with their corresponding colours. I have deliberately omitted a crib-list of associations for each level, as I think it would be an interesting challenge for readers to find out what these might be independently. To scry these levels, I would suggest banishing, entering gnosis, then concentrating on the name of the level whilst looking at a sigilised version of the name. I have scryed each level in a manner similar to the way I scry Enochian Aethyrs, and visionary experiences unfold that have promoted personal growth! I think this illustrates the point that we can chop the 'potato' however we like – into thirty-two pieces, thirty, sixty-four – or twenty-one – but it's the same potato were slicing, and by experiencing each of these 'pieces' we're taking crucial steps toward enlightenment.

I think we need to understand our Higher Self/Holy Guardian Angel in this respect. If our goal is enlightenment and spiritual experience, it is enough for us to acknowledge this for the work to begin. I'm reminded of the remote viewing experiments conducted by the C.I.A. in the 1970s and 80s, where targeting their operatives' visions proved to a much simpler process than they at first thought it would be. Likewise with spiritual exercises. Just knowing that it is growth and development that is sought through inner plane journeying is enough to enable the experience, and what you call the map, and even what the map looks like, will make no difference to the validity of the trip.

I think this all boils down to the fact that in the mind of the Creator time does not exist – everything has simultaneously happened and is happening – and all is One. There is no-one for all the things that have already happened/are happening to happen to. It is just our dusty minds that complicate things by dividing and differentiating, seeing differences and waiting for things that have already occurred. The Enochian Aethyrs, the Tree of Life, and the levels the angel I 'met' revealed to me, all have one thing in common, and that is that they split the One into the many. In doing so, they remind us of the ultimate unity of everything. Division of anything is a reminder that there is a unity to divide.

Namaste.

THE STELLA OF
REVEALING

Jason Bloch was roused from sleep by his alarm clock. He cursed, threw the covers back and swung his feet onto the floor. It was nine o'clock in the morning, and though he didn't have a job – not a mundane, earthly job, anyway – there was much he had to do that day. Moving into the kitchen, he opened the fridge door – the portal to the icy realms. On the lower shelf – Malkuth – was half a loaf of bread; above it, in Yesod, was half a bottle of wine, lying on its side; the third shelf up contained nothing but oranges. The top and last shelf was the fridge's Da'ath, and in correct Sephirothic fashion, it was impenetrable and mysterious. Not because of spiritual veiling, but because it held several plates of mouldy food.

'Forgot to buy milk again,' Jason grumbled, slamming the door shut.

A few minutes later he was dressed and ready to go out to the corner shop. Jason stopped when he got to the front door. The postman had thrown the morning's post through the letterbox, and he felt compelled to divine the day's events from the pattern the fallen letters created. Kneeling down he quickly went into a light trance. *The spiritual battle quickens today. My nemesis is abroad, and seeks to harm me. Must remain vigilant. Much at stake.* Jason shook himself from his trance, but retained the memory of what he had discerned. He was not surprised by the letter-portents. Every day for Jason Bloch was a battle between Good and Evil.

'Good morning, Raj,' Jason said as he entered Raj Patel's store a few minutes later.

'Good morning, Jason,' Raj said, beaming cheerfully. Looking around to check that they were alone, the man added, 'Those magazines you asked me to order have arrived. Do you want me to put them in a bag for you?'

Jason reddened. He was conducting some very important

research into Babalon, and was annoyed that Raj thought he wanted the pornos he had ordered for masturbatory pleasure. It was hard work, tracing the Scarlet Goddess' shifting influence through the British media, and he didn't like his efforts being misunderstood. *They understand little; judge them not.*

'Yes Raj, put them in a bag. And can you tell me where your tissues have moved to? Can't see them here.'

'To your right. By the lady towels.'

On the way home Jason ran through the things he had to do that day. That afternoon he had an appointment at the job centre, where patient Mr Mellings had been trying for over a year to encourage him to get a job. After that he was going to call in at his Mum's. He hadn't seen her for over a month, and his finances were suffering as a result. Finally, tonight The Order of The Shining Ring, of which he was Grand Master, was meeting at his place. Jason's chief enemy, Mr Kirkpatrick, was stirring up trouble for him and his Order, and before the evocation they had planned, they were going to have to talk about how to thwart the threat he represented.

It began to rain. Jason wiped moisture from forehead, transferring it to his lips. 'Element of Water,' he intoned solemnly.

Unfortunately, so enraptured was Jason with his adoration of this element that he took his eyes of the footpath, tripping on a rupture in the pavement and toppling to the ground. He bashed his head heavily on the pavement. 'Element of Earth,' he said croakily as he got to his feet.

Worried about what surprises the fire element might have in store for him, Jason ignored the urge to smoke as he carried on unsteadily home.

Later, as Jason was browsing in a bookshop to kill time before his job centre interview, he began to wonder whether his fall earlier that day had left him mildly concussed. He felt slightly unsteady on his feet, and had a splitting headache. He wandered into the Children's section, and found himself looking at an illustrated book featuring Disney's Pluto character. Looking at the dog, with its goofy expression and big eyes, Jason found himself overcome by a sense of Oneness with the animal.

'I have chosen you,' he heard Pluto say.

'Me?' Jason said loudly, making a small boy in dungarees look at him in surprise.

'Yes, you. You need to buy me.'

'Buy you? But you're a cartoon character.'

The boy's mother walked over and led her son away by the hand.

'You need to buy the book you're looking at.'

'Oh.' Jason picked the book up and looked at it closely. 'Pluto In Egypt' it was called, and the front cover showed Pluto standing proudly in front of the Great Pyramid of Giza. Peering around the side of the pyramid was a fox, who was looking slyly at Pluto. Jason took the book to the counter and paid for it, using a bag containing coppers to come up with the four pounds ninety-nine pence it cost. After he had left the shop Jason put the book in his shoulder bag. 'Don't talk to me when I'm with Mr Mellings,' he instructed the volume as he walked off. 'We can't have *him* knowing about talking books.'

* * *

'So, Jason, how have you been getting on with your job search over the last couple of weeks?' Mr Mellings, fiftysomething and with a kindly face, tapped a pencil on his chin as he waited for Jason to answer.

'Well, you know how it is,' Jason replied, glumly. 'There just aren't many opportunities out there for Hebrew scholars or antiquarian book dealers.'

'We both know that, Jason. But that's why I've been asking you to consider other types of work. You need to be less fussy in what you'll consider.'

'Yes, but as I've said to you before, I have a sensitive temperament. I couldn't work on a building site or in a fast food restaurant. I'd have a nervous breakdown.'

Mr Mellings sighed. 'There are other jobs out there. You could be applying for an administrative job somewhere. You know, office work. No tattooed builders or chip fat to deal with.' Mellings looked down at a sheet of paper on his desk, then said, 'Look, we had this vacancy come through this morning. It's for an administrative assistant in a marine insurance firm. Now that might suit you.'

Jason wrinkled his nose. 'I have a master's degree. I couldn't possibly consider working with a bunch of spotty and illiterate eighteen-year-olds.'

'Jason, you don't know who you'd be working with until you at least go for an interview. And even if you *were* working with younger and less qualified people than yourself – well surely that's better than vegetating in front of the television all day . . .'

'I do no such thing! I'm a very busy person . . . !'

'But not busy looking for a job it would seem,' Mr Mellings said. 'Jason, you have signed a Jobseeker's agreement, but you don't seem to be adhering to its conditions. Now will you let me put you forward for interview at the insurance company?'

'No.'

'Well then, I have to tell you that if you can't provide evidence of having been actively looking for work when we meet in two weeks I will have to consider suspending your Jobseeker's Allowance . . .'

Mr Mellings continued to lecture Jason, but the latter had become distracted by Pluto's insistent voice. *I will come unto you tonight. You have been chosen.*

'. . . so will you do that for me?' Jason heard Mr Mellings saying, but Pluto had totally ruined his concentration and he didn't know what the older man was talking about.

I will come unto you tonight. You have been chosen.

'So will you?' Mr Mellings said, impatiently.

I will come unto you tonight. You have been chosen.

'Yes, come unto me tonight!' Jason said, audibly.

'What?' Mr Mellings said, puzzlement evident on his face.

'Not you,' Jason said. 'Pluto!'

'*What?*'

Thoroughly embarrassed, Jason rose to his feet. 'Don't worry, ignore me. I'll see you in two weeks. I have to go now.' With that he walked out of the office as quickly as he could.

When Jason got back to his car a traffic warden was standing in front of it, in the process of issuing him a ticket. 'Hey, mate!' Jason shouted. 'I can't be more than two minutes over my hour!'

'Rules is rules,' the warden said, not bothering to look up from his handheld ticket machine.

'But I'm unemployed,' Jason whined. 'Come on fella, give me a break.'

'No can do.'

'So how much is this gonna cost me?'

'Forty quid if you pay it in two weeks, seventy if you don't.'

'Ah, that makes sense,' Jason said, suddenly sounding more cheerful.

'Yeah, it's an encouragement to pay on time.'

'No, I'm not talking about that. גזל – Hebrew for 'rob' or 'plunder' enumerates to forty – the same price as the ticket if it's paid on time. And נהיה – Hebrew for 'wailing' or 'lamentation' – enumerates to seventy. Very apt don't you think?'

'You've lost me, mate,' the warden said, scratching his chin.

'Not altogether surprising. You *are* after all only a traffic warden.'

'Least I've got a job. Here. Take your ticket.'

When Jason got home he had about an hour to eat something and tidy up his temple – otherwise known as the living room – prior to the arrival of his brethren from the The Order of the Shining Ring. He ate baked beans on toast, then got to work. Jason ordinarily stayed up late watching DVDs and smoking cannabis in the living room, and he very often fell asleep there, so there was a week's worth of pizza boxes, crisp wrappers, socks and coffee cups full of butt ends to clear up. When all the rubbish had been cleared out, he vacuumed, then lit several joss sticks to remove the lingering odour of smelly socks and tobacco.

On the dot of seven o'clock the first member of The Order rang the bell. Opening the front door, Jason saw that it was Theo – or Frater Hystericus, to give him his magickal name – a pony-tailed computer programmer with a large beer belly.

'How high does the toad jump?' Jason asked

'As high as the beetle flies,' Theo replied.

'Enter.'

Over the next half hour Frater Chilli (Bill), Frater Flaming Pentagram (Bob) and Soror Horror (Jane) all turned up. All members of The Order of the Shining Ring alive at that time were finally gathered in Jason's house.

After everyone had been served tea or coffee, Jason addressed the group. 'As you know, we will be performing an evocation of Ronald Reagan at eight-thirty, but before that there's an important matter we need to discuss – namely, Patrick Kirkpatrick.'

'I saw the article he wrote in The Morning Echo,' Bill said. 'What a cunt.'

Patrick Kirkpatrick had been a member of The Order of the Shining Ring until the previous year, when he had fled the temple half way through his 8th degree initiation ceremony. The man had been totally unprepared to lose his virginity with Soror Horror, a requirement for successful completion of the initiation rite. From that moment he had ceased all contact with Order members. Four months earlier he had set up his own order, The Chaste Knights, of which they knew little apart from the fact that it was headed by Patrick. Worrying developments of late had been that Patrick had begun to use his position as a junior reporter with The Morning Echo to covertly attack Jason, and there were also indications that a magickal attack had been launched.

'Yes, I know,' Jason said. 'He did everything but name me.'

'But how can he get away with this sort of thing?' Jane wanted to know. 'Why don't you just complain to the editor of the paper? Or sue them – even better.'

'It seems someone living on this road is in cahoots with him, and has gone on record as saying *they've* seen someone exposing himself to an old lady,' Jason said.

'It's the description of the man as wearing a red baseball cap that really condemns you,' Bob said. 'I mean, he might as well print your name. That's *you*.'

'I know, I know,' Jason said. He had gone slightly red, and

hoped the others didn't notice. 'I mean, fancy exposing yourself to an *old* woman. Who would do that?'

'You should go to the police,' Bill said.

'They've already been to see me.'

There were gasps from the others.

'Yesterday morning,' Jason continued. 'I think they were talking to everyone that lives on this road.'

'What time was this?' Jane wanted to know. 'I was here until almost eleven.'

'They knocked on my front door just after you left.'

'You were . . . you were wearing your red cap yesterday!' Jane said. 'Did you have it on when they spoke to you?'

'Yes. Yes I did. But don't worry. I told them it wasn't me, and I think they believed me. Anyway, let's not dwell on what's happened. We need to decide what we're going to do about Kirkpatrick. I'm thinking we might need to summon a Goetic demon to constrain him.'

There was an intake of breath by Bob. 'You know what happened last time we tried that. It's heavy shit.'

'The problems we had last time had a human cause,' Jason said.

'You *say* that, but I think it was the demon working through us,' Bob countered.

'*You* knocked the candle over,' Jason snapped. 'And that was before we'd even started.'

'Yes, but remember how quickly the room caught on fire,' Bill pointed out.

'That's because sheets are very flammable!' Jason said angrily. 'Sheets will burn if you apply fire to them. '

'Poof!' Bob said. 'From tipping the candle over to having the fire brigade spraying the house seemed little more than ten minutes. I think the demon had his hand in it.'

'Well, we do our rituals without candles nowadays,' Jason said. 'And you . . .' Jason looked at Bill, '. . . you can make sure you come properly attired. If the demon *did* cause our problems last time it was probably because you came dressed for the working in jeans, T-shirt and flip-flops. How would you feel if you were a demon and someone dressed like that was trying to summon you?'

'There aren't many ceremonial magicians around these days,' Bill said. 'If I were a demon I'd be glad that someone was showing an interest in me. Think how little attention they've had since the Middle Ages!'

'You cretin,' Jason said. 'Do you think the Goetic demons are sitting around in a lounge somewhere, waiting for humans to page them? They roam the world, seducing, tempting and influencing. We're not doing them a favour by calling on them.'

'Demons have feelings, too,' Jane said, looking warmly at Jason. 'We should trust Jason on this one. He *is* the Outer Head of our Order, after all.'

Taking encouragement from this remark, Jason said, 'Yes, you can take my word for it about needing to meet demons' minimum requirements regarding decorum. So no jeans or flip-flops. Now the question we need to consider is which demon to summon . . .'

The group discussed this subject for several minutes, without reaching agreement. Matters were not helped by Bob's insistence that there was a recently discovered demon called Hipsorinkle, a fact the others disputed vehemently. Eventually Jason called an end to the debate, instructing everyone to don robes for the evocation of Ronald Reagan. 'Let's move swiftly,' he instructed. 'I want to catch Newsnight at ten-thirty.'

By just after eight-thirty the group had all changed into green robes, and were gathered in a circle in the temple. Electric torches had been placed at the four quarters, each standing on its base and casting a circle of light onto the ceiling. Since their episode with the fire, they had incorporated the torches into their ritual paraphernalia as a safety measure. To accommodate their desire for magickal appropriateness, each torch had been painted black, before being adorned with silver magical symbols. After a thorough banishing that involved the sprinkling of chilli power around the perimeter of the circle, Jason stepped up to the altar. It had been adorned with a black and white photograph of Ronald Reagan as a young man, a card that bore the words 'Evil Empire' and a small Californian flag. 'Oh Ronald, oh Ronnie!' Jason intoned sonorously. 'We call upon you to grace us with your presence. Appear before us!'

All members of the Order directed their gaze at the white triangular piece of board that had been placed outside the circle. On it stood a brazier which was sending forth a steady stream of smoke.

'Oh, Ronnie,' Jane implored in a quavering voice. 'Come to us!'

'Only I can address the spirit!' Jason hissed sharply.

'Sorry,' Jane mumbled.

'Don't say anything,' Jason said. 'You're breaking my concentration.' Raising his arms above his head he continued, 'Ronald! Guardian of the Modern World, Bringer of Freedom, Man of Diplomacy, come to us! Come to us!'

Jason lapsed into silence for some time, then whispered, 'Ronald, I see your outline. Is that you? If it is please give me a sign.' Silence again, then, 'Thankyou Ronald. I see the golden arches of McDonalds. Symbol of dining convenience from your home country. You are with us.'

Jane whined softly. Bob cleared his throat. Bill just looked at the triangle of manifestation with unwavering concentration.

Jason slipped into glossolalia, voicing words that sounded vaguely Arabic for several minutes, before falling silent. Then: 'Ronald,' Jason said in a tone that suggested both reverence and familiarity, 'we have brought you forth today because as a group we desire wisdom. Impart your gift of discernment to us so that we may better live our lives. I have opened my psychic channels. Communicate with me directly.'

Jason placed his hands to his temples and dropped his head. After a few moments he started to issue a strange guttural gurgling, which then turned into words: 'Pluto will help you. Pluto loves you. Look to Pluto. Pluto hates those damned Russkies. Pluto. Plutonium. Remember to drive on the right. Stay to the right. The right wing. The right wing sings. Galahboohkarabalongi. Marigolds. Simbantoopinghatrimonko. Say 'hi' to Margaret. Great legs. She could have tied me up anytime she liked.'

Jason began to sway, and seconds later he collapsed in a heap on the floor.

Jane rushed over to him. 'Are you okay?'

'I told you not to talk during the ritual,' Jason mumbled. 'But yes, I am.' Getting to his feet he said. 'Ronald has spoken to us. Let us now banish, after which we will analyse his message.'

* * *

The next afternoon Jason and Frater Hystericus were sitting in the Rose and Crown, sipping bitter while they waited for a prospective new member of the Order to show up.

'Ten minutes late,' Jason observed.

'He might be here but hasn't looked in this alcove,' Frater Hystericus said. 'From the bar it isn't obvious that this area exists.'

'If he is a true aspirant he will find us,' Jason observed solemnly. 'A true aspirant would not be put off by a . . . corner.'

'I guess not,' Theo said. 'Did he say what he'd be wearing – or did you give him descriptions of us?'

'I said that I would be with you, and that you have long hair and are quite fat.'

'You said *what*?'

'Well, you *do* have long hair, and you *are* fat.'

'Maybe so, but you could just as easily have said that I was six foot five. That's also true, probably more likely to distinguish me from other drinkers, and . . . and it sounds better.'

'I knew we'd be sitting down. It's hard to judge the height of someone who is seated.'

'My beer belly isn't very obvious when I'm sitting down, either.'

'Okay, okay. Whatever. It's too late now. He'll find us if he's meant to find us.'

'What do you know about the guy?'

'Not much. Just that . . .' Jason broke off and raised his right hand to his right ear, bending his head to the side.

'Trapped nerve?'

'No. It's Pluto. He's . . . he's talking to me again.'

'What's he saying?'

'Something about Disney. Disneyland near Paris. I'm getting pictures now. Wow . . . Images of a can in a lamppost near one of the rides. This relates to my spiritual destiny.'

'Here,' Theo said, sliding a ballpoint pen and newspaper over to Jason. 'Maybe you should be writing this down.'

Jason picked up the pen and began scribbling. After a couple of minutes he stopped and looked up at Theo. 'There's going to be more tonight. Jesus, this stuff is dynamite!'

'What have you got so far?'

Jason opened his mouth to reply, but just then a young, skinny, teenager with blond hair walked up to their table and said, 'Hi. Are either of you Jason?'

Jason looked at the youth. He seemed younger than the seventeen years he had given as his age. There was a delicacy about his face, his mouth especially, that made Jason wonder if he was gay. 'Marcus?' Jason said. Without waiting for an answer he pulled a chair out: 'Take a seat.'

'I'll get them in,' Theo said, rising. 'Bitter?' he said, looking at Jason, who nodded. 'What can I get you?' Theo asked Marcus.

'Just bring me an empty glass,' Marcus replied.

Theo's brow creased in confusion. 'An empty glass?'

'I don't want anything to drink, but I find the act of holding an empty cup quite symbolic. It suggests to the universe that I'm a receptacle that wants to be filled.'

'Or an idiot that deserves to be killed,' Jason said. 'I don't really mean that,' he added quickly. 'It just happens to rhyme.'

Marcus looked at Jason suspiciously, but appeared to allow the remark pass.

When Theo returned from the bar Jason cleared his throat dramatically and said, 'So, Marcus . . . how can we help you?'

'Well, I've been interested in the occult for ages. Ever since I first read a Harry Potter book. I feel now is the time to take things further. I heard about you guys from Sally's best friend's son, and I've seen your pamphlets in Mystic Moon bookshop.'

Jason and Theo exchanged looks.

'What sort of magickal work have you done up to now?' Jason asked Marcus.

Marcus rubbed his nose briefly, before replying, 'Well, I've read all the Harry Potter books. They were good. Then I read a book on affirmations – you know, saying stuff over and over, and then it happens. I tried affirmations to get noticed, because for as long as I can remember people have always ignored me . . . and it worked!' Marcus shifted in his chair. 'Yeah, people started noticing me and paying me so much attention. By the end I was repeating the phrase "you will be seen and noticed" over and over again – pretty much all day – and people were looking at me, really seeing me for the first time!'

Jason remained silent for a few moments after Marcus had stopped talking, then said, 'Our concept of magick has nothing to do with Harry Potter. That's just fiction – stories for kids. Affirmations *can* be useful – if you repeat something a thousand times it may well seep into your subconscious and result in a kind of reprogramming. But again, that sort of thing isn't really what we're all about.'

'That's fine. That's why I've come to you guys. I want to learn. Teach me!'

'Well, that's a possibility . . .' Jason conceded.

'I meant to say, I've got a green belt in karate. Does that give me a head start? Can I come in at a higher grade 'cos I've done martial arts?'

Theo shook his head, a look of dismay on his face. 'This isn't like a college course where you get credits for previous study. You're not working towards a GNVQ!'

'I guess I've got a lot to learn. So, can I join?'

'You can consider yourself a *potential* candidate,' Jason said. 'We need you to fill this form in,' he slid a piece of paper across the table, 'and post it to the address at the top.'

Marcus glanced at the form briefly, before nodding. 'Okay. I should be able to get this off to you tomorrow morning.'

'Don't rush it,' Theo cautioned.

'I won't, but I will get to work on it straight away.'

'Cool,' Jason said. He was about to ask Marcus whether he was currently studying, when suddenly an incredibly tall, thin man loomed over their table. 'Marcus!' the man said. 'Are you of an age to be drinking in a pub?'

Marcus swung around to see who was talking, then said, 'Oh, Carson . . . what are *you* doing here?'

'This is where I spend most afternoons. What are *you* doing here?'

'Um. Just . . . just meeting some friends . . .'

'But you don't have any . . . I mean, aren't you meant to be working at that newsagent?' Turning to Jason and Theo, Carson said, 'I'm Marcus' stepfather.'

'Mother's boyfriend,' Marcus corrected.

'Yes, well, however you want to put it.'

'I'm not working this afternoon,' Marcus said. 'I never work Thursday afternoons.'

Carson pulled a seat up and joined the table. 'So you're friends of Marcus?' he said, looking at Theo and Jason.

Jason found the situation very awkward. He and Theo were at least fifteen years older than Marcus. After all the fuss in the paper over the flashing, the last thing he needed was an accusation of kiddie-fiddling. 'We . . . uh . . . we . . .'

'You look green,' Carson said. 'Like my Uncle Freddie when he was suffering from tyrotoxism.'

'What's tyrotoxism?' Theo said.

'Food poisoning caused by cheese.'

'Oh . . .'

'Why are you here all the time?' Jason asked Carson.

'I'm an alcoholic. It's my job to spend a lot of time in places like this. But forget *me* – you haven't answered *my* question. Are you guys friends from school? There seems to be a bit of a . . . bit of an age gap. Mind the Gap! That's what they say, isn't it Marcus?'

Marcus went bright red – almost as red as Carson's alcoholic beacon of a face. 'These guys are members of a . . . group. A group I'm interested in joining.'

'A *group*?' Carson vocalized the last word as if just pronouncing it left a bad taste in his mouth. 'A *group*? Would this be a music *group*? Or perhaps a theatrical *group*? Or maybe even a *group* of lizard collectors?'

'It's a magickal group, actually Carson.' The effort of saying this seemed to exhaust Marcus, who closed his eyes briefly and began to sway slightly in his seat.

Carson turned to look at Jason and Theo. 'What the fuck is going on here? I'm a nuts and bolts sort of guy a – gradgrind – and someone who understands fully how furciferous young Marcus can be. Now, if this is some sort of paedo thing you've got going here, I only ask that you leave immediately. We'll all pretend none of this ever happened. If you *not* paedos, then I want a full explanation, and pronto.'

'No, we *are* members of a magickal group,' Marcus said.

'Is this some sort of Harry Potter appreciation society?' Carson said. 'Do you all dress up as wizards and warlocks and pretend to turn each other into toads? Cavort with drazels in smoky rooms?'

Jason giggled nervously. 'Magick is maybe a confusing word to use – it just makes people think of fairytales. Perhaps to say we're a group of spiritually-minded people would give a better idea of what we're all about.'

'Not a cult, then?' Carson said with a twinkle in his eye. 'You don't prey on people who are having an attack of the mulligrubs? Seduce them with promises of happiness?'

'Certainly not,' Jason said.

'So what's in it for you?' Carson wanted to know. 'You must have an angle here.'

'If we have an angle, it's spiritual advancement. If your stepson becomes involved with our group he will certainly not be asked for monetary donations, or expected to behave in a sexually inappropriate way – in *any* sort of sexual way. Now, if you don't mind, I think we should get back to the matter at hand – interviewing Marcus – without yourself as audience.'

'Well, that's as firmly put as I could ask for, to be sure. I guess I'll just wander back to the bar and deal with my eternal polydipsia.' Carson turned to look at Marcus. 'Keep your eyes

peeled and your ears open, boy. I trust you'll use all the common
sense you have in dealing with your new friends.'

Marcus nodded. Carson sauntered off. Jason looked at
Marcus.

'Sorry about that,' Marcus said. 'He's been a total idiot for as
long as I've known him.'

'I didn't understand half of what he was saying,' Theo com-
mented.

'He's got this thing about big words. He thinks he's the bright-
est person alive, and he's learned all these big words no-one ever
uses. By using them he thinks he's proving how smart he is, but
most people don't even notice 'cos they're not listening to him
in the first place.'

'If he's as smart as he thinks he is you'd think he'd do something about his drinking problem,' Jason said.

'Oh, no, he's really proud about that,' Marcus said. 'He thinks
the only response someone as clever as him can have to living
in a world full of normal people is to be drunk all the time. He
thinks it helps him come down to our level.'

'Idiot!' Jason snorted. 'How can *he* possibly . . . ,' Jason
stopped mid-sentence, an expression of horror frozen on his
face. After a few moments his lower jaw began to work, as if
he wanted to say something. Finally, he began to speak, but
not in his normal voice; instead of his regular reedy Estuary
English accent, the voice that emerged sounded robotic and
more American than anything. Jason sounded like an angry
Dalek. 'The Stella of Revealing is in the Disney of Paris. You
must travel there. You will find it in the lamppost, by the Wild
Western Runaway Train ride.'

Marcus looked at Jason with an expression of awe. 'Wow.
You totally zoned out there. That was amazing! Was that some
real magick?'

'This Pluto character you're channeling seems to be pretty
insistent,' Theo observed. 'How seriously do you think we
should be taking these messages?'

'I don't know. He sounds like a confused Thelemite. The Stele
of Revealing I know all about, but the *Stella* of Revealing? That

has to be some sort of joke. You drink from this can of magic beer and all is revealed?'

* * *

That night Jason encountered Pluto in his dreams. The crazy dog was leading him through the Eurodisney Park, striding so quickly Jason had difficulty keeping up with him. Children looked at Pluto adoringly and waved as the pair marched past, but the great dog totally ignored them.

'It is important that you remember everything I am showing you,' Pluto said to Jason.

'Why is that?'

'So when you come here in reality you'll be able to find what I'm about to show you.'

'What do you mean "when you come here in reality"?'

'Well, you're dreaming right now.'

'I am?'

'Yep.'

'Everything seems far too vivid to just be a dream,' Jason said.

'That's because your dream has just turned lucid.'

'It has?'

'Yep.'

'Oh, yeah. There aren't the normal anomalies I'd expect in a dream, though.'

'You're talking to a dog aren't you? What more do you want?'

'I guess . . .'

'Here we go . . . ,' Pluto said. The pair were approaching a Wild-West-themed roller coaster which soared behind a plastic façade of cacti and gunslingers. A snake of queuing park-goers spilled out from the entrance – it looked like the person at the back would be in for a hell of a wait. Just in front of the attraction was a lamppost, and Pluto walked right up to it, then bent down. At the bottom of the post was a small door, which opened sideways on hinges. Pluto opened the door, and pulled out a can of Stella lager. 'This is it,' the dog said. 'The Stella of Revealing.'

'It's a can of beer . . .'

'Yes, but a can of beer with a difference. Drink from this can and you will be immediately propelled across the Abyss.'

'Why are you showing me this?' Jason asked. He was briefly distracted as a small child suddenly doubled in size, then popped and disappeared. 'I mean, this is a dream. I can't drink anything in a dream.'

'That's true,' Pluto conceded. 'But what I'm showing you exists in real life. I want you and one friend to take a trip here in your normal waking life – to come to Eurodisney. I want you to come here and drink from this can. You, my friend, have been chosen.'

'But why me? And what for? Who *are* you anyway? Disney characters aren't meant to be spiritual guides.'

Pluto smiled at Jason but didn't say anything. Jason opened his mouth to speak some more, but the dream faded, and suddenly he found himself in his bed, with a right arm that had gone totally numb because of his sleeping position.

An hour later Jason was on the phone to Jane, telling her about his night vision. 'I just don't know how seriously to take it,' Jason said. 'It sounds absurd, but as I was dreaming Pluto seemed totally believable.'

'I think you need to assume this is a genuine message,' Jane counseled. 'You *are* the Outer Head of our Order. You have to accept that this sort of thing could happen to you.'

'True. But Eurodisney is a long way away. I'll feel like a total idiot if I go all the way there and find nothing.'

'You'll feel like an even bigger idiot if you don't go and you later find out you missed out on the spiritual opportunity of your life.'

'True . . .'

After finishing his phone call, Jason walked over to the mirror in his living room and looked at his reflection. He didn't see the face of a spiritual avatar staring back at him, but he was coming to the realization that that was what he might one day be. He had been chosen. Chosen by Pluto.

Such thoughts excited him, but also made him tense. And tension . . . well, he only really had one way of relieving that.

Hating himself for his weakness, but almost overwhelmed with anticipation, Jason raced upstairs to his bedroom. Quickly undressing, he slipped on a long woollen greatcoat that had been draped over the back of a chair. He yanked a pair of muddy Wellingtons onto his feet, and put a tweed flat cap on his head. Ray-bans completed his strange look.

Jason headed outside. He was worried about the Wellingtons. They would slow him down if he had to run, but if he wore normal shoes it would be obvious to anyone he encountered that he wasn't wearing trousers beneath the coat. He didn't want to create any more suspicion than he had to. The day was mild – far too mild for his clothes. It hadn't rained for over a week, making the boots seem a very odd choice of footwear.

Jason scuttled to the end of his road, turned right, and then walked down Mitchell Street toward the park. He figured there'd be a few women out walking dogs there. He could surprise one of them, as long as their canine companion didn't look like the type to put its jaws around his member. Just before he reached the park he passed Gladys Holcombe, who lived two doors down from him. She had been one of the neighbours who had been particularly vocal in suggesting a citizens' patrol of their street to protect against the flasher. Jason averted his gaze, hoping the hat and sunglasses were enough of a disguise.

Strolling through the park, Jason saw that he had been correct about the dog-walkers. Apart from a couple of joggers, everyone seemed to be holding a leash. Hating himself for being in this position – *yet again* – but thoroughly excited, Jason looked around for a likely target. It couldn't be anyone with children – sexual deviant he might be, but he had some standards. In the distance Jason could see a woman crouching by a large oak tree. She seemed to be doing some stretches – either before or after a run he guessed. There was a gate near the spot the woman was occupying. This was looking promising. A means of escape was something he always had to bear in mind. Not that he normally had to run following a flashing. His victims normally did the running.

Nearing the woman, Jason saw that she was an attractive brunette in her mid thirties. *Perfect*, he thought. He took a glance around to see who else was in the vicinity. No-one was within a hundred yards. 'Arise, arise ye pole of wonder!' Jason intoned. There was a stirring in his groin that indicated his pole of wonder was indeed stirring. 'Arise ye member of majesty, as I rend the veil of my robes, may Babalon recoil in wonder!'

Jason was now right by his target. 'Aiiieee!' he shrieked. The woman turned to look at him, and at the same moment Jason opened his coat, revealing his bobbing erection.

'Jason, what on earth are you doing?'

Jason froze. This was not going to plan at all. How did this woman know his name? Arms still holding his coat open, he looked more closely at his victim. He *did* know this person. It had been a long time, but he knew her. He broke into a cold sweat as realization dawned. It was Sally Cartwright. They had been at primary school together. This woman was still a close friend of his sister, Lucy. He shut his coat as if vigorously drawing a pair of curtains.

'It *is* you, Jason, isn't it?'

'Yes. I mean no.'

'It is you! You haven't really changed that much . . .'

'I . . . I . . . I'm sorry. I shouldn't be doing this . . .'

Sally stood up. 'You're right. You shouldn't be. But don't worry. I understand you're suffering from a compulsion you can't really control. I'm not going to call the police or anything.'

'You won't?'

'No, of course not.'

'What about my sister. Are you going to tell her?'

'If you promise to see someone about your . . . your condition, then no, I won't.'

Memories of the time Jason had spent in Sally's company as a child returned. The effortless way in which, quite unintentionally, she had made him feel inferior and grubby. Sally had always been so perfect. Perfect in appearance, always getting perfect marks, ever perfectly behaved.

Jason could feel himself getting another erection, and decided it was time to go. 'Well,' he said. 'I'm off. I appreciate you not saying anything. I *will* see someone.'

'You take care, Jason.'

* * *

When Jason got home he felt quite wretched, almost tearful. The thought entered his head that he should ring one of the members of his Order up and confess all about his . . . his urges. He decided against this, however. They needed him, and to have them lose faith in his spiritual authority for no reason other than his need to unburden himself seemed selfish. Instead he decided to summon Babalon another way.

He got onto the internet and made straight for fuckfest.com. Scanning the thumbnails on the 'Milf' page, he looked for a suitable Babalon. In his mind she had to be of a Mediterranean hue, with a well-pronounced figure – and most importantly, have something of the night about her. He found it hard to describe exactly what he was looking for – the best way he could put it was a darkness in the eyes, a curl of the mouth and a posture of aggressive abandon.

Halfway down the page he found her. The thumbnail showed a large-breasted and big-buttocked woman, crouched on all fours, her backside directed temptingly upwards. Her eyes looked like black holes, drawing the viewer toward her with a magnetic pull. Jason clicked on the picture, and soon a video filled the screen.

'Ah Babalon!' Jason squealed a few minutes later, releasing 10cc of body fluid. 'In nomine Babalon, Blessed Be. Whew!' He stood up, his jeans hanging around his thighs and walked to the bathroom.

Jason sighed deeply as he stood under the warm jets of the shower. His wank had relaxed him totally, and he now didn't even care that he'd flashed Sally in the park. His thoughts turned to Pluto as he soaped his body. It was quite apparent that he *would* go to Paris. The only things he had to decide were when, and with whom. Jason decided that he should go soon, within a few days if possible. The dream hadn't suggested that the Stella of Revealing was only going to be in the location shown for a finite time, but he didn't want some drunk coming along and taking a swig from the can. Sooner was definitely better than later. As to whom to bring with him, the obvious choice seemed to be Jane; it would look a bit strange two men in their thirties going to Eurodisney. He was having enough of a struggle controlling his flashing instincts – he didn't want people to think he was a kiddie-fiddler. He decided to go straight over to her place and sound her out.

It took Jane so long to answer the door when Jason banged on it half an hour later that the latter almost gave up and left. Finally she appeared, looking as if she'd just got out of bed.

'Jason . . . ,' she said. 'Wasn't expecting to see you this morning.'

'I need to chat to you,' the man replied, walking past her into the hallway without invitation.

'Come in,' Jane said sarcastically, before turning and following Jason.

'I need you to come to Eurodisney with me,' Jason announced when they were both seated in the living room.

'Me?'

'Yes, I've thought about it, and I think it will look more normal if I'm travelling with a woman.'

'Who's really going to care? People who go to Eurodisney go for the rides, not to look at other visitors.'

'Maybe, but I'd just feel more comfortable. So will you come?'

'I'm a bit skint this month. I don't know, Jason.'

'You're skint every month, as am I. However, this is important enough that I'm willing to dip into a little reserve fund I have. I'll pay for you.'

'Well, that puts a different complexion on things. Count me in!'

* * *

That evening Jason was sitting in his habitual spot – the sofa – with the television on and a half-eaten pizza on the coffee table in front of him, when he suddenly started to feel odd. At first he thought he was going to have a panic attack – he'd been plagued by them in his late teens; he was experiencing the same tightness in his throat, clammy hands and elevated heart rate – but the sensation was somehow different. Jason wasn't fearing for his physical health as he used to during a panic attack; it was his very soul that seemed threatened. He got the impression that just out of sight was a huge cosmic vacuum cleaner, one that was heading straight for him and would soon suction him up and out of existence. Jason looked around the dimly-lit room, lights flashing on the walls as the television picture changed, and wondered what was going on. A thought occurred to him. 'Pluto?' he said. 'Is that you?'

There was no reply, but the sense of foreboding, of impending annihilation, grew stronger. Jason thought about getting stuck into a bottle of Jack Daniels he had in the house, but that would mean going upstairs to his bedroom, and he feared leaving the living room. There was a duvet lying on the floor beside the sofa, and Jason picked this up, threw it over his head, and lay down on the couch. This simple act of self-protection made him feel worse, however; not being able to see who was in the room with him made him feel there was sure to be another entity present.

Throwing off the duvet, Jason sat up and reached for his mobile phone, which was lying on the coffee table. Who could he ring? His father was dead, his mother went to bed at dusk, and his previous girlfriend had been married to some wanker for almost ten years. He wanted to ring an Order member, but didn't want to lose face with any of them. Jason remembered a friend of his who had a drinking problem saying that the Alcoholics Anonymous helpline was a real lifesaver, that the staff manning it were always really understanding. He would ring them, he decided. He felt confident that he could bluff a drinking problem. Ten minutes on the phone with one of their counselors and his strange feelings might go.

'. . . so how long have you been drinking, Jason?' the woman's voice was warm with concern.

'I guess since I was about fourteen. But it's been in the last two or three years that things have gotten really bad.'

'You drinking every day, darling?'

'Pretty much.'

'My drink of choice was wine,' the woman, whose name was Sandra, said. 'Towards the end I was getting through two or three bottles a night. I'd stopped eating. Job? Forget it. I just forgot to go in to work one day, and that was that. They never saw me again, and never got an explanation. Luckily I was married at the time, or I'm sure I'd have ended up homeless and sleeping under a bridge somewhere.'

This sounded pretty ferocious to Jason; he'd have to raise his game here if he was to pass as a real alcoholic. 'Yeah, well recently I've taken to filling the bath with white wine. Just getting into the tub and scooping booze into my mouth. And the shampoo bottles I would empty and fill with vodka, and when I wasn't scooping wine into my mouth, or submerging myself and just opening my mouth, I'd be swigging spirits from the shampoo bottle.'

Sandra paused before replying to this comment of Jasons'. 'Jeez sweetheart. I've been an AA member for almost twelve years, but that's about the most decadent, full-on drinking tale I've heard. Have you been in a wine bath today?'

Emboldened by this response, Jason replied, 'No, not today. I've just woken up, but I have a vague memory of being at a party in a squat where they were pouring surgical spirits into a bucket, mixing in some Fanta, and then everyone was drinking out of the bucket with straws.'

'I really think you need to attend a meeting today. Do you think you're ready to stop drinking?'

'I think so. I've got a splitting headache, and my mouth tastes vile.'

'I don't mean just today, I mean are you ready to give up drinking full-stop?'

'I guess so. I'm here at home on my own at the moment, and I'm feeling a bit weird.'

'That'll be the withdrawal, darling. How long has it been since your last drink?'

'Um . . . about six hours.'

'Mmm. That's kind of soon for withdrawal to start. But it could be that.'

'I feel sort of scared . . . ,' Jason admitted. He could scarcely believe he was being so frank. Strangely, he had now almost come to believe he *was* an alcoholic, so wrapped up was he in this dialogue. 'You couldn't come over and hang with me for a while, could you?'

'Well, that wouldn't be appropriate, Jason, would it? Besides, I have a shift to work. If I'm not here, I'm not answering the phones.'

'I just feel so wretched,' Jason said. A wicked thought popped into his head. 'I'm worried I might start drinking again.'

'Well that's the worst thing you could do. You need to go to a meeting. Let's see, its ten past seven. What's your postcode?' After Jason had provided this information Sandra hummed to herself for a few seconds before saying, 'Yes, here we go. Eight o'clock at St Michael's church, Padstow Road. Is that far from you?'

'Not so far.'

'Well there you go then. Get yourself off to that meeting. You'll be with other alcoholics, hearing about how they're coping with their disease. And you'll be distracted by company. You're not going to feel lonely or scared in a room full of other people.'

'I guess . . .'

Some time later Jason shuffled into the church hall, looking around anxiously lest he spot anyone he recognize. He couldn't believe he had actually come to the meeting, but in truth, though he wasn't an alcoholic, coming had at least got him out of the house and distracted him from his feelings of oppression. He hoped by the time he got back home he'd have totally forgotten about his earlier episode, and would be ready for a good night's sleep.

The meeting was brought to order by a burly Irishman in his mid-forties who looked like he'd seen the inside of a prison cell. 'I'm Gerald, and I'm an alcoholic,' the man said. This was stating the obvious, Jason thought. 'Welcome to the Friday evening

St Michael's meeting. Alcoholics Anonymous is a fellowship of men and women who share their experience, strength and hope with each other that they may solve their common problem and help others to recover from alcoholism . . .'

Jason saw analogies with this preamble and a Lesser Banishing Ritual. Setting the scene, clearing the mind. Maybe he could pick up some tips here, even if he didn't need to stop drinking.

After a reading of the Twelve Steps – plenty of occult significance in the number twelve – Michael outlined the format of the meeting, then said: 'Can I ask if we have any newcomers amongst our number tonight? I ask so they may be afforded the same welcome we received when we first attended an AA meeting.'

Jason went bright red. A couple of attendees glanced in his direction, obviously aware of his status as newbie. Jason looked intently at his hands, but his peripheral vision indicated he was still being stared at. Finally he looked up, cleared his throat, and said, 'Yeah, I'm Jason. Thanks for having me.'

A murmur of greeting rippled through the room. 'Thanks,' Jason said. 'Pleased to be here.'

'Yes, you're very welcome,' Gerald said. 'Now I'd like to introduce today's speaker, Jamie. Jamie, you and me have known each other for years, and we've both seen each other when we were really sick, sick with this disease we call alcoholism . . .'

Jamie, wearing a Panama hat and looking like a hung-over pimp, nodded.

'. . . so it gives me great pleasure to know you today when we're both well. And we're well today through this amazing Fellowship called Alcoholics Anonymous. So let me hand the meeting over to you. We all look forward to hearing you speak today.'

'Thanks, Gerald.' Jamie settled further back into his seat; he looked like he was trying to get comfortable in preparation for a short nap. He pulled at the front of his hat, then continued, 'Those of you who have been around for a while will have heard my story many times, but I really don't tire of telling it.

To remind myself of where I've come from – the change in me from then to now – is something I need to do as often as possible . . .'

Jamie spoke in a low mumble; he sounded like he was about to drift off. The delivery was in sharp contrast to his message.

'. . . but today I'm going to vary things slightly and focus on something that obsessed me when I was drinking. It may seem a strange thing to concentrate on, but I hope it illustrates the madness of this disease. When I was in active alcoholism my drink of choice was Stella lager . . .'

At this point Jamie made eye-contact with Jason. Jason gulped. The man continued to stare at Jason as he continued his story.

'. . . Stella. Quite apt this beer bears a woman's name, because I had a love affair with her. I should mention that the beer is actually named after the Latin for 'star', but whenever I hear the name I think of a beautiful woman with hair the colour of the brew . . .'

Jason looked away from Jamie, staring at the ceiling for a few seconds, but when he returned his gaze Jamie locked-on to him straight away. *This is fucking weird*, Jason thought. *First the dream with Pluto, now this guy banging on about Stella.* He felt like he'd wandered onto the set of a crazy film, without anyone bothering to point this out.

'. . . so anyway, I was so into my Stella, I'd get through up to fifteen cans of the stuff everyday. I loved those white cans, the way moisture droplets would whizz down the side of them when you pulled one out of the fridge on a hot day. Then when they were empty you could piss into them if you couldn't be bothered to get up and go to the toilet. That may sound disrespectful, but I saw pissing into an empty Stella can as something like making love to it. You know, my body fluids going into the receptacle the can is . . .'

Now Jason was starting to get really freaked out. He wanted to leave, but thought it would look really rude if he walked out in the middle of the guy's talk. *Why do I care? They're just a bunch of piss-heads.*

'. . . one day I was really pissed, and I decided to make a suit out of empty Stella cans. I had about a hundred empties scattered around my house and I gathered them all up and threw them in my bath. I ran half a bath and rinsed out all the cans, then left them to drain by placing them upside down on the bathroom floor. Came back an hour later and started attaching cans to a pair of overalls by hooking big safety pins around the pull-caps. I even put pennies in some of the cans, so if I shook my ass there'd be a proper racket.

'I had a gram of coke at home, so after I'd put on this ridiculous outfit I snorted a couple of huge lines. I downed another couple of cans of Stella, then left my place. I don't know if any of you have seen pictures of those African witchdoctors that cover themselves in a sort of straw costume, so you can't see practically any of their body. Well I was like that, except with cans instead of straw. I'd decided I wanted to go on a "pilgrimage" to the off-licence I used to buy most of my booze at. You should have seen the looks I got from people as I walked along the street. Talk about the Tin Man! That was me, clanking along, with a mixture of water and beer dribbling from a lot of the cans. At one point I passed a policeman, and he gave me a long hard stare, but what could he do? Being crazy isn't a criminal offence. I wasn't stumbling too badly, and I wasn't swearing at anyone.

'Finally I get to the offie. I walk in and it's quite busy for the time of day. One of the girls serving I know quite well – girl called Tanya I used to flirt with. She doesn't know what to make of me as I start circling the shop, occasionally stopping to shake my body like a dog trying to dry itself. All the other customers start looking at me. After I've walked around the shop about three or four times I suddenly flip out. I don't know about you, but occasionally I have these strange thoughts in public places. You know, I might be in a bank, and I'll think, "What would happen if I just pulled my pants down here and ran around screaming?" Well, on this occasion, instead of just thinking about it, I actually did it. Just went berserk. First I ran over to where all the cans of Stella were, and pulled them down off the shelf. Then I went over to this cardboard cut-out of a woman and start ballroom dancing with it around the shop, before throwing it at a customer. I picked up cans of Guinness and started throwing them at the wine section, smashing a bunch of bottles, and knocking a lot of them onto the floor. I started picking up broken bottles of wine and pouring whatever liquid remained in them into my mouth, staining my face and neck red so I looked like I been in a fight.

'Eventually, after I'd done probably several thousand pounds worth of damage, I fled the shop. My way home involved a walk up a fairly steep road, and I was about halfway up this when I heard sirens in the distance. I hoped it might be a fire engine or something, but guessed it probably wasn't. The siren got louder and louder and I figured it was a police car on its way to pick me up. I was passing a Woolworths at this point, and for some stupid reason decided to go into it. I was hardly going to be able to avoid being spotted given what I was wearing, but I was too pissed to realize this . . .'

Jason froze when he heard mention of the man storming Woolworths. *He* had been in the store when this had happened. This had been years before. Jason guessed he couldn't have been older than seven or eight. A vivid memory returned of turning into the stationery aisle, and seeing a beer-can-clad man running toward him. He'd been with his aunt, and they had clung to each other, frozen to the spot, as Jamie had clattered past, pursued by an overweight security guard. He could remember the guard's cap flying off as the men rushed past.

He and his aunt had left the store straight away, and Jason could still remember the conversation that ensued, as he had demanded to know why Jamie had been behaving in the way he had. Notions of drunkenness and insanity were totally alien to him at that time, and he had asked a lot of questions his aunt had struggled to answer. Now, thinking of the tale he'd just heard – the strangeness of having witnessed part of the story, and of the dreams he'd had that involved another can of Stella – he felt as if he was being stalked by destiny. He'd left the house to escape weirdness, only to find even more weirdness. Jason stood up. Only a couple of people glanced at him as he left the room.

Back at home he was sufficiently intrigued by the whole Stella angle to have forgotten his earlier fear. Jason pulled a can of Heineken from the fridge – he was quite pleased it was Heineken – and settled down in front of his computer to do some research. Typing 'Stella beer' into his search engine of choice, he was quickly presented with a list of websites relating in some way to the Belgian beverage. Clicking on the manufacturer's site, he read a brief history of the beer. The brewery that produces it – AB InBev – can trace its roots back to 1366. Stella Artois itself was first produced in 1926 and named after the star of Christmas. 'Interesting,' Jason said aloud. 'Every man and every woman is a star.' Looking at the beer's logo, he noticed the cornucopia that forms an integral part of it. 'Even more interesting,' Jason murmured. He was aware of the origins of the cornucopia as a symbol. In Greek legend, Zeus had been raised on the breast milk of a goat named Amalthea, in a cave on Mount Ida of Crete. 'Baphomet?' Jason mused audibly. Halfway down the webpage was an advert for 'The Chalice', a stemmed beer glass in the shape of a truncated egg. Babalon? Jason asked himself.

Standing up, Jason picked up his can of Heineken and walked down to the living room. He began to pace. Was the guy at the AA meeting delivering him a message? Or was he going mad? Were Pluto and the Stella of Revealing, and everything else he thought he'd discovered in his magickal career just symptoms of a mental illness only he and a few other similarly affected individuals were unaware of? He thought about taking himself off to Casualty, to be assessed, but his other bright idea of the night had resulted in him becoming more confused, and he was scared of who or what he might encounter if he stepped outside his front door. But he didn't want to be alone with his thoughts, especially considering where they were leading him.

An idea eventually came to him. He took all the cans of beer from the fridge and plonked them on the living room coffee table, then went upstairs and retrieved the bottle of Jack Daniels. An hour later Jason was staring blankly at two television screens, mouthing words he wasn't listening to. Finally he fell asleep, his hand still clenching an empty can of beer.

* * *

Two days later, at just after seven o' clock in the morning, Jason and Jane pulled out of Kings Cross station. The speed and efficiency of the service made Jason feel he had been transported to France the second he stepped aboard their Eurostar train. Landscape whisked past them as they accelerated toward the Channel Tunnel, and after what seemed like little over half an hour they were beneath the sea. Emerging in France, Jason observed that an alien would not immediately notice the differences between this country and the one they had left behind; northern France was green like southern England, the cars broadly similar, the people similarly dressed. If there was a difference, Jason decided, it was the strange angles at which smaller objects were positioned with respect to larger objects. Small cars parked near a larger truck would typically be at an angle of around forty-five degrees, whereas in England that would more likely be parallel or bumper-to-tail. The same thing seemed to apply to people he saw standing on railway platforms or in the street. The smaller people were at strange angles to the larger people.

Half an hour after emerging in France, Jane started slapping herself on her temple and mumbling words that Jason couldn't catch. She was performing this action every few minutes, drawing stares from other passengers.

'What *are* you doing?' Jason hissed at his companion after he'd decided he couldn't ignore this strangeness any longer.

'It's a little ritual I have,' Jane replied. 'Whenever I travel to a new country I have to slap my head and say "Yes, Mr Cobino" until I see a yellow car.'

'Well, *don't*. You're embarrassing me.'

'I have to. The only time in the last ten years I didn't do it the friend I was travelling with was mugged and almost killed.'

'Oh, come off it!'

Jane slapped her forehead. 'Yes, Mr Cobino.'

'Stop it!'

'Do you want to get mugged?'

'No . . .'

'Well then. If you're embarrassed you can help me look for a yellow car.'

'We're passing fields. We're not going to see one in a field.'

'Be patient.'

Finding it hard to believe he was joining in with this nonsense, and wondering whether he should have asked one of his other Order members to accompany him, Jason began searching for a yellow car. He winced every time Jane slapped herself, but managed to resist shouting at her.

They were approaching the outskirts of Paris before a yellow car was spotted. Jane jumped up in her seat when she saw it, giving Jason such a fright he spilled coffee down his T-shirt. Nevertheless, he was pleased he didn't now have to worry about being mugged. They passed through grim council estates that were the match for the worst Jason had seen in England. Burnt-out cars and smashed windows attested to recent rioting.

'Almost there,' Jane observed.

'I should have booked a train that took us to Eurodisney directly, but we have an hour's wait after we get to Gare du Nord before our connection.'

'Gives us time for lunch . . .'

After alighting from the train Jason and Jane walked out of the station so they could smoke. As they puffed a gypsy woman walked up to them and said, 'Speak English?'

'Canberra is the capital of Australia, but Sydney Australia's most populous city,' Jason replied. 'How's that for some spoken English?'

The gypsy responded to Jason's statement by putting her hand out, palm up, in the universal begging gesture. Jason slapped the hand, then put his own hand up as if he expected to be hi-fived. 'Put it there,' he said when she didn't respond. The woman looked at him blankly, then muttered something in her own language and wandered off. Jane looked at Jason. 'My turn to be embarrassing,' he said by way of explanation.

Three hours later they were standing in a line, waiting to check in at their Wild-West-themed Eurodisney hotel. Children raced around the lobby excitedly, high on sugar and Disney, as their parents queued to pick keys up or drop them off.

'I wonder what a real cowboy from 1850s Montana would make of this place,' Jason said as he looked around, taking in the abundance of wood, the moose's head hanging from a wall, and the nineteenth century fittings.

'Bemused. Confused. Pissed off with these kids.'

'I wonder if there'll be a hotel here in two hundred years that's themed on 2010 Europe,' Jason said.

'Dunno . . .'

'I somehow doubt it. We're not doing anything extraordinary at the moment. We're not conquering new lands or worlds, or flying around in spacecraft. We're just getting old, and fucking around with computers.'

'What do you mean "we're just getting old"?' Humans haven't just invented ageing.'

'No, I know,' Jason said. 'But the average age of Europeans is just going up and up. There have never before been so many elderly people alive.'

'That's not a *bad* thing . . .'

'I'm not saying it is . . . I guess this place is quite authentic in some ways. Its *authentic-phony.*'

'What's that supposed to mean?'

'Well, as a society, we're a bunch of phonies. We live in mock-Tudor houses, and play at being Japanese for fifteen minutes when we eat sushi at lunchtime. We collect "friends" on Facebook that we've never even met, and get more worried about cardboard characters in Eastenders than members of our own family. We're phonies, and here we are, right at home in our phony Cowboy hotel.'

'I think you need a drink.'

By the time they had deposited their bags in their room, it was just after five in the afternoon, and both Jason and Jane were feeling tired. 'What do you want to do?' Jason asked. 'Check out the park?'

'We could do. But it'll be getting dark soon. Maybe we should get an early night and be up first thing tomorrow.'

'I'm not going to argue with that suggestion,' Jason replied with a grin. He threw himself onto the bed and switched the television on. 'Good old CNN. I never feel I've left England until I'm watching CNN in a hotel room.'

'How often are you away from England?' Jane said. 'You make it sound like you're a proper jet-setter.'

'I guess I haven't done much travelling recently,' Jason conceded. 'But I used to. When I was working as an accountant I used to take two or three short holidays a year . . .'

'*You* were an accountant . . . ?'

'Yeah. I had to quit after I got into the occult. I kept converting numbers into their gematriacally corresponding words. Working with numbers all day it got a bit much. In fact it gave me a nervous breakdown.'

They ate that evening in one of the restaurants that was part of their hotel complex. In keeping with the Western theme it resembled a huge barn, and contained a large stage on which attractive cowgirls sang country numbers to entertain the diners. The food was served buffet-style, and was French-influenced Tex-Mex. Refried beans and Tacos with baguette.

'I'm fucking starving!' Jason said, as he sat down with a huge plate of food.

'You got enough there?' Jane said sarcastically as she looked at Jason's towering pile of chicken wings, potato salad, ribs and marinated mushrooms.

'Yep. But I don't rule out going back for seconds. Have you noticed we just forgot to have lunch? I haven't eaten since this morning, and that was just an apple.'

'I'm hungry as well, but I'll just have to see how much of this Country and Western music I can stand. It goes right through me. Makes me ill.'

'Wouldn't buy it, but it doesn't bother me.'

'So what are we going to do tomorrow, exactly?' Jane said, talking with a very full mouth.

'Well . . .' Jason speared a couple of mushrooms and popped

them in his mouth, '. . . we turn up nice and early. We want to get there before it gets too busy. Then we locate the ride that I saw in my dream. Like this place, it's some sort of Wild West thing – should be easy to find. Then I retrieve the can of Stella I'm expecting to find from a big street lamp.'

'What are you going to do with the can when you find it – *if* you find it?'

'That I don't know yet. I'm hoping I'll get some inspiration when I'm holding the can. I mean, once I have it we're done here. We can hang out in the park for a few hours if you want, or go straight back to Paris and have a look around there. Our train back leaves Gare du Nord at ten past seven, so we've got a while to kill.'

Feedback from the microphone on the stage made them both wince, interrupting talk.

'Please, enough of that music,' Jane said, looking with annoyance in the direction of the stage. 'I hope they're done now.' Returning her gaze to Jason, she went on, 'Are you going to drink the can if it's got liquid in it?'

'Yeah – of course. Worst that it can contain is bum's piss, and the best – well, it could be the Elixir of Life, the Mead of the Gods. Actually, I've got an idea. Let's do a spot of receipt divination.'

'What's that?'

'Watch and learn,' Jason said. He pulled his wallet from his pocket and began to rifle through it for receipts. When he had a small pile of pieces of paper in front of him he put his wallet away. 'So let's see. Newspaper and confectionary two days ago at W.H.Smith. Total cost £3.33. Wow. 333 is the sum of the Hebrew word for 'snow', and if we sum it we get the number nine, attributed to Yesod, the Sephirah of, amongst other things, illusion. So we're being told *it's no illusion*. We're on the right track.'

'Hang on. I get the Yesod bit, but where are you getting 'it's no' from?

'Duh,' Jason said, rolling his eyes. 'Snow – *it's no*. They're practically the same sound.'

'If you insist . . .'

'You dare to doubt the ancient art of gematria!' Jason was grinning.

'It just sounds like mental masturbation to me. I prefer the physical type, to be honest.'

Half an hour later the pair were sitting in the hotel's bar, having what was intended to be a single drink before retiring for the night.

'This feels . . . strange,' Jason announced, after a sip of his lager.

'In what way?'

'It's almost as if we're a couple. You know, room together, having dinner and a drink like this . . .'

'Well, we're not. I hope you're not expecting any hanky-panky when we get back to the room.'

'No, I wasn't,' Jason said defensively. 'But it wouldn't surely be the worst idea you'd ever heard if I was.'

'Well, no . . .'

'I mean, you're no beauty queen, yourself.'

'Is this your idea of seduction?'

Jason shook his head. 'I don't know what I'm saying. To be honest I feel a bit strange.'

And indeed he was. Just in the past few minutes he'd begun to feel hot and light-headed. Sounds seemed to be coming from down a long corridor, and colours seemed a lot brighter.

'Are you coming down with something?' Jane asked, pleased the discussion had moved on.

'I don't know. Maybe.' Jason rubbed his eyes. 'I guess we've had a busy day . . .'

But the way Jason was feeling had nothing to do with their busy day, and everything to do with the mushrooms he had eaten with the evening meal. In amongst the harmless button and chanterelle mushrooms contained in the salad had been large quantities of Fly Agaric, slipped in by a disgruntled employee who had been loudly reprimanded twice by his boss in the preceding two weeks for not washing his hands after using the bathroom. At that very moment an ambulance was on its way to their hotel from the nearby town of Lagny-sur-Marne, having been called by staff who had been alerted by other guests to the strange behaviour of an elderly grandmother, seventy-eight year old Elsa Cummings. She had been shouting warnings to an invisible person she had addressed as Pluto, and had started throwing bread rolls and bananas at the entity, before being restrained.

Ten minutes later Jason was slumped on the bar, resting his head on his arm. He looked like he was slowly melting.

'Jason, let's go back to the room,' Jane said, shaking his shoulder.

'Urgh?'

'Come on, let's go.'

Jason stood up, but his legs felt like jelly. The walls of the room were pulsating as if he was in the belly of an organic creature. 'I think I'm tripping,' he said, before breaking into a giggle.

'Have you taken something?'

'Not that I know of. Maybe I've been spiked.'

'Let's get you back.'

A smile spread across Jason's face. 'Not so fast. Let's go and look at the stars a minute.' He led them through the main lobby area, and out the door.

'I'm not sure that's a good idea,' Jane said. 'Come on. It's a bit late and a bit cold for star-gazing.'

Jason stared up at the sky. There was heavy cloud cover, stained a yellow colour by the street lamps that illuminated the approach to the hotel, meaning there were no stars to see.

'No stars visible,' Jane said. 'Come on. Let's go.'

Ignoring his companion, Jason wove drunkenly in the direction of a grassy slope that rose on the other side of the road, allowing himself to collapse when he reached it. He rolled onto his back and stared skywards.

'Look, I'm not hanging around here with you,' Jane said impatiently. 'If you feel ill I'll call a doctor, but I suggest we just go back so you can sleep this thing off. Have you forgotten about the can of Stella? You have to be awake to try and find that tomorrow.'

Jason didn't reply. He was making an undulating, snake-movement gesture with his hands, staring at them intently as he did so.

A woman wearing hotel staff uniform approached them. She said something to Jason in French, but too quickly for him to understand her. Taking them for English simpletons she pointed at Jason, then showed an upturned palm to gesture 'What's-going-on?' This Jane understood. 'Sick,' she said. 'Il est malade.'

'Doctor? You need doctor?'

Jane shook her head. 'Not yet. I take him back to room,' she said slowly.

The woman nodded. She gave Jason a concerned look, then walked away.

'Oh, wow . . .' Jason said, looking in the direction of a car park.

'What is it?' Jane said.

'Oh, wow wow wow! He's here!'

'Who's here?'

'Pluto. But he's a many-armed Pluto. A Kali-Pluto. And in each arm he has a can of Stella. Oh, shit. This is all about tomorrow.'

Jason stood up and lurched in the direction of his vision. Jane followed. 'I've had enough of this,' she said. 'You could trip and fall in your condition.'

'Condition? Who's fishing in my condition? I'm swishing my lishing. You wanna see my lishing?'

'I'm going back,' Jane said.

'Can I show you my lishing if I come back with you?'

Jane didn't reply. She turned and started to walk away.

Jason ran after her. 'Pluto says I can show you my lishing. Do you wanna see it? You can touch it if you're gentle.'

'Fuck off.'

'I'm offering you my lishing!'

Jane sped up, eventually breaking into a run. Jason followed after her for a few moments, but then pulled up sharply. He could hear Pluto-Kali calling him. Turning around he saw him-her standing before him. He-she had grown, and now stood ten feet tall. The entity's eyes glowed with a phosphorescent brightness, and the Stella logo on the many cans of beer he-she held had a neon glow, as if actually lit with electricity. The creature's arms began to move more and more quickly, like a huge organic Ferris wheel. Jason tried to keep the cans of beer in focus, but as the speed of movement increased they became nothing more than an electric blur. Finally there was what sounded like a gun-shot, and Jason lost consciousness.

When he awoke, weak sunlight showed that dawn was breaking. For a second Jason was confused as to *who* he was, let alone *where* he was, but slowly memories of the previous night returned. Groaning, he got to his knees and rubbed his eyes. Had Jane left? How had he ended up tripping his nuts off the night before? Getting to his feet, he brushed leaves from his clothes and began to walk in what he hoped was the direction of his hotel block. He was right in his hunch and reached the door of his room soon after, knocking hesitantly. The door opened quickly to reveal a pale-looking Jane. 'You're alive . . .' she said, without much relief.

Jason barged into the room, and collapsed onto the bed. 'Fuck I'm knackered.'

'Where were you?'

'Thanks for sending a search party out after me,' Jason said, ignoring the question.

'I wasn't worried about you. I have great faith in your sur-vival abilities. What happened?'

'I think I must have just passed out. I woke up in a little stand of trees. God knows how I've avoided hypothermia – or even managed to sleep.'

'Well we know what happened to you, anyway . . .'

'Apart from meeting God . . .'

'No, there was a note pushed under the door this morning. Apparently anyone who had the salad with mushrooms in it from the restaurant last night was in for quite a treat. Laced with magic mushrooms. They're urging anyone who thinks they might have had some to contact reception so they can be checked out.'

'A bit late now.'

'You should go. You might be able to get some compensation.'

Jason grunted. 'The trip could pay for itself, even before we get the can.'

'How are you feeling now?'

'Spaced out. I'm getting some visual distortion, but nothing major. Not compared to last night, anyway.'

'So you're going to be okay to go to the Park?'

'Yep. Just as soon as I've had a coffee and seen the hotel doctor.'

* * *

Jason's heart was beating rapidly as they queued for the turnstiles that accessed the park. It was just after nine in the morning, but hundreds of other park-goers had risen early in a vain attempt to beat the crowds. *The pilgrims at the gates of the palace*, Jason mused, taking in the faux-Gothic turrets and ramparts that rose above them. He had always wanted to go to Disneyland as a child, and now, twenty years into adulthood, he was finally getting his chance. He looked at Jane, who had a smile on her face as she took in her surroundings.

Once in the park proper they followed the general course of the crowd, walking slowly and grinning unashamedly. 'Look, there's Snow White and the Seven dwarfs!' Jane said, grabbing Jason's arm. Off to their left a float that resembled a huge silver chariot carried the eight fairytale characters. Children and parents surged forward to photograph them as they passed.

'I'm shitting myself,' Jason announced.

'Why?'

'I'm suddenly convinced we're not going to find anything.'

'That's not a reason to shit yourself. You'd be disappointed, but . . .'

'Yeah, but I'll look like a real dick if this turns out to be a waste of time.'

'You'll look a little bit silly to four or five people if there is no can. I don't think it will make the headlines.'

'You're putting my magickal aspirations in perspective, that's for sure.'

'Ego is the biggest obstacle to magickal obtainment, so you should thank me.'

'Jane, I'm beginning to think I've really underestimated you. You don't always say a lot, but what you do say is more often than not worth hearing.'

'Don't be so condescending! My self-worth isn't dependent on your opinion of me.'

'No, of course not. Ignore me.'

'Do you have any idea where the ride we're looking for is? We should have picked up a map.'

Jason stopped walking abruptly and turned to face Jane. 'I've decided. I'm not going to look for this can. I can't bear the thought of it not being there. Let's just go back to Paris. I can always tell myself it was here, and I just didn't have the courage to look for it.'

'You bloody chicken!'

'But I don't think I could cope with finding out this was all a load of rubbish.'

'And supposing the can is there, and picking it up, or drinking from it, does the most wonderful things to you – enlightens you, or whatever? You would risk missing out on that because of the temporary silliness you'll feel if it's not there?'

Suddenly Jason had an overpowering urge to streak in the grounds of Eurodisney. His customary stress-release mechanism was kicking in. Looking over Jane's shoulder, he saw a tall brunette with breasts threatening to burst from her blouse, and could contain himself no longer. 'I need to go to the toilet – like now!' he announced. 'Have you seen any loos?'

'Over there,' Jane replied, pointing at a single-storey building forty metres away.

Jason ran toward the toilets. Jane followed at a walk. He walked straight into a cubicle and started to take of his clothes. When he was fully naked he stopped and realized he faced a problem – he didn't have a flashing mac. He could either just streak totally unclothed, or improvise a flashing outfit. He decided it was too cold to go totally naked, and he wanted some way of preserving his modesty when he was, as he would be, finally apprehended. In the end he put his shirt and jacket back on, along with his shoes and socks. His privates were wonderfully exposed, but he put his trousers back in his shoulder back so that he could put them on when the need arose. A man was just walking in to the toilets as Jason emerged from his cubicle, the latter starting in fright as he saw Jason's lack of attire. Jason grinned at the man. 'I thought you Froggies were relaxed about nudity!' he said. The man rushed past him and locked himself in the cubicle Jason had just vacated.

Jason took a deep breath as he stood by the toilet exit. He felt like an Olympic ski-jumper, just before launching himself down a huge slope. With a shout of, 'Yieeahhhiii,' he burst out of the building, almost colliding with a pair of elderly sisters. Luckily for them they were too short-sighted to notice that Jason's penis was on display. A woman who had very good eyesight shrieked as Jason brushed past her, his member shaking from side to side like a crazy metronome. This outburst shook Jane from a daydream; she had been unaware that Jason had emerged from the toilets. Her jaw fell open as she saw his bare buttocks moving away from her, people pulling aside to give the Englishman as wide a berth as possible. 'What the fuck?' she muttered to herself. *This better be the drugs he took*, she thought, but at the same time she remembered the fuss that the flasher had been causing in Jason and Jane's home town. *Could they be the same person?* She decided to follow after him at enough of a distance to not be obviously associated with him, whilst staying close enough to see when he was apprehended.

Jason, meanwhile, was becoming overcome with endorphins and sexual charge. Wherever he looked he saw women – small women, big women, young women, old women, attractive women and pig-ugly women – but all women! And all unable to keep their eyes off him. His excitement was further heightened by the knowledge that the fun must end soon. Security surely already knew he was running amok; men would shortly be dispatched to bring his run to an end.

Jason continued to sprint through the crowd. Out of the corner of his eye he could see that quite a few people were filming his progress. He ran towards one man who was wielding a digital camera. 'A bit more interesting than Daffy Duck, hey mate?' he shouted as he passed him. 'Check out my boner!'

For indeed, Jason was now sporting an erection. As he continued to run, weaving and ducking as he attempted to avoid colliding with other park-goers, Jason caught sight of someone running toward him who looked familiar. Who was it? Another hotel guest? No-one had made enough of an impression for him to remember them, especially in the state he'd been in the night before. He looked again, and suffered a shock of recognition at realising it was Marcus from England!

'Marcus!' Jason shouted as they neared each other. 'What are you doing here?'

Marcus looked at Jason in horror. 'Where are your pants?'

'A long story. Come on, run with me. This is your initiation!'

The boy fell in next to Marcus, trying to stifle the embarrassment of being near the older man.

'We're going to get nabbed soon,' Jason said through deep breaths. 'So we need to run like we've never run before. Nothing should happen to you because you're dressed. I might get arrested, but it shouldn't be a big deal.'

'Okay.'

'How did you know that I was here, anyway?'

'Theo sent me. He thought you might need help.'

The crowd roared with delight and disgust as the pair continued their course. Out of the corner of his eye Marcus saw a blur of blue. Turning his head, he saw that it was a policeman in pursuit, and that the man had two colleagues close behind him. Jason increased his speed, but he could feel he was beginning to tire. A huge queue for a Peter Pan ride snaked in front of them, but split into two as he and Marcus neared. As he passed through the gap created a fat man with baseball cap threw an ice cream at them. It landed squarely in Jason's face, temporarily obscuring his vision in one eye.

Jason wiped ice cream from his face, then glanced over his shoulder. The policemen were gaining on them. 'Keep close,' he shouted to Marcus, before darting into a fast food outlet. 'Hey, who's for a hot dog?' Jason shouted, jiggling his penis. 'Free hot dog!' Jason exited before he could catch anyone's reaction. He had reached an area of the amusement park that contained a number of gift and souvenir shops. He entered and exited several of these quickly, hoping to lose his pursuers. Jason tripped as he left the last shop, falling heavily. Marcus was at his side a second later, helping him to his feet. 'Quickly,' the boy said. They ran on, but now the policemen were only a few feet behind. Jason turned right past an information centre, and was suddenly confronted by a sight he had seen before. He'd arrived at the Wild West Runaway Train ride – a tame roller coaster ride that swooped and rose between plastic rocks and mine apparatus. And there, right in front of him was the lamppost from his dreams!

Jason ran straight to it, fumbling with the hatch that was at the base – just as he'd seen in his vision. The policemen had caught up with them, and Jason could see he had no more than seconds before he was apprehended. 'Hold them off me,' he yelled at Marcus.

Marcus nodded, though Jason didn't see this. His attention was focused on the hatch. If it was locked he was fucked. Luckily it wasn't, and though stiff, he managed to pries it open. There inside, as he'd hoped if not expected, was a 500ml can of Stella Artois lager. He could hear Marcus scuffling with someone behind him. He didn't have time to waste. Grabbing the can he saw that it was already open, but it felt like it contained at least half of its volume in liquid. He felt a hand on his shoulder, and immediately lifted the can to his lips. Hoping fervently it didn't contain brake fluid, he began to drink.

The moment the liquid touched his palate it felt as if a nuclear bomb had detonated in his brain. At the same moment as this happened, Jason *became* the liquid. From being a semi-naked man drinking from a can of lager, he became 91 centilitres of Belgian beer, cascading down a throat. Then he became Jason's stomach. Then he became everything, and nothing, and everything and nothing. And Everything. And Nothing.

APPENDIX 1

The twenty-one levels of spiritual attainment, as revealed to me by the Angel I encountered in the Atlas mountains

Level 1	Kremion	Colour: Muddy brown
Level 2	Sarphal	Colour: Bright orange
Level 3	Mensour	Colour: Pale green
Level 4	Caerphil	Colour: Strawberry red
Level 5	Simmium	Colour: Pale yellow
Level 6	Portens	Colour: Dark, menstrual red
Level 7	Haspur	Colour: Navy blue
Level 8	Arjens	Colour: Greeny-yellow
Level 9	Kimmium	Colour: Silver
Level 10	Berac	Colour: Dirty orange
Level 11	Herstwil	Colour: Light brown
Level 12	Sinkum	Colour: Dark purple
Level 13	Gammas	Colour: Pink
Level 14	Cadiens	Colour: Neon blue
Level 15	Serpens	Colour: Tropical green
Level 16	Telmium	Colour: Sky blue
Level 17	Cora	Colour: Light red
Level 18	Bensentiens	Colour: Light grey
Level 19	Wessler	Colour: Ruby
Level 20	Idiems	Colour: Gold
Level 21	Choralin	Colour: White

BIBLIOGRAPHY

Butz, Jeffrey J. *The Secret Legacy of Jesus.* Rochester: Inner Traditions, 2010

Casaubon, M. *A True and Faithful Relation of What Passed For Many Years Between John Dee and Some Spirits.* London: D. Maxwell, 1659

Crowley, A *The Equinox, Vol I #2.* Simpkin, Marshall, Hamilton, Kent & Co. Ltd, 1909

Denning, M. and Phillips, O. *Mystical States of Consciousness.* St. Paul, MN: Llewellyn, 1985

Denning, M. and Phillips, O. *Vodoun Fire.* St. Paul, MN: Llewellyn, 1979

DuQuette, L. *Enochian Vision Magick.* San Francisco: Weiser, 2008

DuQuette, L and Hyatt, Christopher S. *Enochian World of Aleister Crowley: Enochian Sex Magick.* Tempe: New Falcon Publications, 1991

Goswami, Amit *The Self-Aware Universe.* Tarcher, 1995.

Hey, T. and Walters, P. *The New Quantum Universe.* Cambridge: Cambridge University Press, 2003

Houck, R. *The Astrology of Death.* Gaithersburg: Groundswell Press, 1995

Leadbeater, C.W. *The Astral Plane.* London: Theosophical Manuals, No. 5, 1900

Leary, T. *Exo-Psychology.* New York: Weiser, 1979

Lisiewski, Joseph C. *Ceremonial Magic & The Power of Evocation.* Tempe: New Falcon Publications, 2004

Scerri, Eric R. *The Periodic Table.* New York: Oxford University Press, 2007

Temple, R *The Sirius Mystery.* London: Sidgwick and Jackson, 1976

Tyson, L. *Enochian Magic For Beginners.* St. Paul, MN: Llewellyn, 1997

Zalewski, P. *Golden Dawn Enochian Magic.* St. Paul, MN: Llewellyn, 1990.

www.ingramcontent.com/pod-product-compliance
Lightning Source LLC
Chambersburg PA
CBHW030932090426
42737CB00007B/396